Wealth Flight

Wealth Flight

The Impact of the Housing
Market Value On the Overall
Change of a Community and
How Public Policy Can Help

Monica D. Shepherd, Ph.D.

Strategic Book Publishing
www.sbpra.net

For information about special discounts for bulk purchases, please contact Strategic Book Publishing, Special Sales, at bookorder@sbpra.net.

ISBN: 978-1-68235-937-2

Acknowledgments

The research for this project started decades ago while I was an undergraduate student when I first read the book *American Apartheid* by Douglas Massey and Nancy Denton. While I consider the book a masterpiece, I found many questions unanswered largely due to my own excessive analytical mind. The same critical thinking that caused me problems with teachers as a student in essence benefited me as a researcher and professor. Some people are often considered a problem or oblivious because other people just haven't caught up to their level.

Life experiences are always the best teachers in which there is no degree, publication, or university that can have more value, and thus many of my investigations for this book came from my travels to Detroit, Chicago, East St. Louis and the greater East and West Coasts. What is most important about what I have discovered is that urban issues are not linear, and a majority of the concerns overlap and intersect. I am a historian; therefore, this book has a strong historical pull. Yet, it also includes additional content that revolves around sociology, psychology, economics, and leadership. I focus on leadership because this research is not geared toward highlighting social problems without providing any solutions. I make a point to discuss what has been presented in the past, why the research is valid or invalid, and then allude to what can be done to improve the circumstances later in the book.

Many people have influenced my work over the years. All are equally important because I have always made a point to learn something from everyone I meet because everyone has value. I am a follower of the teachings of Jesus Christ. In fact, the unhoused or dipsomaniac person that gets ignored every day in the community has more insight and intellect about what is occurring in the area more than the philosophical academics who come in with degrees, questions, and laptops (with aims at making a name for themselves) because the former is attentively observing daily and observation is a systemic method.

Digressively, I was fortunate to work with Librarian Barbara Levergood decades ago and her enthusiasm for government documents still inspires me to this day. I am forever indebted to Drs. Jessica Harris and Anthony Cheeseboro. You two hung in there with me and I will always use you as an example when I coach my students through the hardships of academia. Students grow and develop and how they start out will never be how they end. Students should never be dismissed. Special thanks to Dr. Jane West. I truly appreciate your character. Much appreciation to Dr. Olivia Boggs. You inspired me. I believe we crossed paths for a reason. You influenced my scholarship but more importantly my character.

Finally, thanks to my family. Influence and guidance begins in the home.

For Dad!

Table of Contents

Introduction

The aim of this narrative is to provide readers insight into the social association and economic variables that relate to the disparity that affects low-income communities. Low-income communities rarely begin as low-income environments, and when these communities are described as such, often these areas are considered small-town communities. The information that follows will focus on working-class communities that at one time were thriving towns but due to socioeconomic change points presently are consisted low-income or disadvantaged. The intent is to bring attention to the factors that created the shift and how these change points can be remedied to help these towns, cities, and their educational systems.

Past literature on this topic has addressed components solely associated with economics, psychology, or racial discrimination as catalysts for community downturn. Although these components are independently important, this research intentionally combined the challenges that can serve as reasonable intersecting variables for reasons why stewards of place would benefit low-income communities. Throughout this book, I will use the term *disadvantaged* to refer to individuals who live in under-resourced communities. Sociologist William Julius Wilson emphasizes the weight of the term well throughout his decades of research, and although I do not wholly agree with his early work on poverty in Black communities, in essence disadvantaged as an expression brings awareness and recognition.

The purpose of this book is to interlock the differing experiences that relate to social and economic gaps that occur in low-income communities and explain how these problems can be alleviated. These problems tend to manifest covertly prior to visibility. Therefore, I intended to widen the scope of knowledge on the topic and expose a variety of hidden obstacles. The pages that follow will discuss socioeconomic models that can be applied to communities to aid these environments prior to their change point.

CHAPTER 1

What is Wealth?

Financial wealth ensures equity. In its simplest form, it can be reduced to what designates an asset from a liability. Income is not wealth but rather financial earnings. Net worth is the outcome of one's assets after measuring liabilities (debt). Household wealth is measured by the housing market value because housing market value/home ownership is a predictor of wealth based on equity availability. Equity is an economic asset upon which wealth is built since it is generated and increases over time. The general expectation is that property, unlike other depreciating assets (liabilities) such as cars, will gain value over time. Research by Loving et al. (2012) revealed, "Housing value comprises the largest single non-pension component in a household's portfolio, at roughly 35 percent of the median household's wealth" (p. 3). Traditionally, homeownership is the most significant contributor to net worth that is associated with an individual or family at any given time.

Property value can fluctuate because of unfavorable community establishments or curb appeal. In the same way, the presence of a vacant, unkempt home next door or the visibility of an adult entertainment facility can lower property value. Property value is evaluated via assessment, which is usually based on the market value of properties, while property taxes are a result of property assessments. One cannot have a tax rate without first having the property assessed. After all, an individual is not responsible for the taxes on an item until value has been assigned to the commodity. A community's housing market value, more than its property taxes, has a direct association with regional economic trends. Property tax rates occur after establishment of the home value, and property value comes by way of assessment.

For example, for the last forty years, the city of East St. Louis, Illinois, has been a blighted city in the metro-east portion of Illinois. Although this city has experienced its share of social and economic transitions, like White Flight, East St. Louis also has higher property taxes than some of the most affluent communities in the area. East St. Louis shares similarities with other cities that have experienced White Flight, but East St. Louis experienced a habitual increase in its Black population while economic opportunities were simultaneously declining over the years. Once a city of 82,295 residents and named an "All-America City" by the National Civic League in 1959, it has shifted to 18,469 residents as of 2023.

The Total Population of East St. Louis, Illinois: 1940–2017

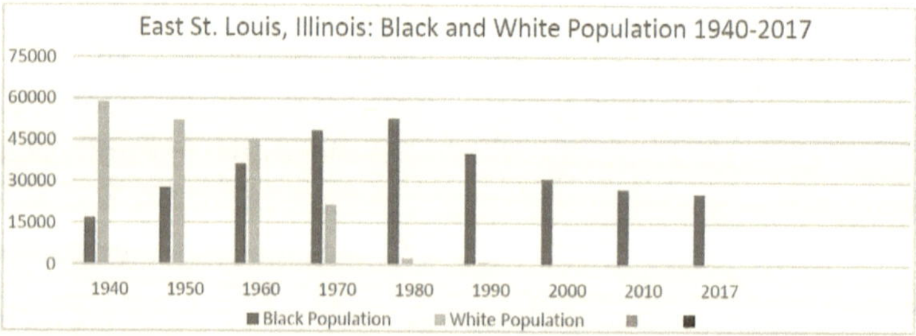

Note: Reprinted with permission from Source: United States Census Bureau of Population and Housing: Summary Population and Housing Characteristics: Illinois. Washington: Government Printing Office.

East St. Louis has the highest property taxes in the area; reports determine that the property tax rate in the area is as high as 20 percent (Landis, 2017). The surrounding, more affluent communities that have school systems with abundant resources have property tax rates lower than 10 percent. Someone who has "a $35,000 home in East St. Louis paid $1,996 in property taxes in 2016 on a 17 percent aggregate tax rate, while owners of a $36,000 home in O'Fallon paid $1,034 on an 8 percent rate" (Landis, 2017, p. 2). Investigations over the years have confirmed that Black Americans have higher property taxes than White Americans and that low-income communities have greater tax bills than more affluent neighborhoods.

Take Flint, Michigan, as an example. Flint has experienced a decline of the automobile industry and has experienced a preventable water crisis. Flint has a poverty rate of 40.4 percent (U.S. Census Bureau, 2019) but yields the highest water bills in the nation (Wisely, 2016). People with less often pay more, and although taxes are important to a community to a certain degree, more attention should be paid to the housing market value trends in the area.

The critical part about understanding home value assessments in relation to community property taxes is that both business owners and residents pay community taxes. The ultimate aim for most city governments is to keep community taxes at desirable levels in order to attract enterprises to the location. Although the number of prosperous firms in a community is an indication of regional income, housing market values are better barometers for assessing community trends. To clarify, housing prices in many communities will fluctuate because of the school system. Yet, many examples can correlate that homes are less expensive in cases where community schools have struggles, but when this is the case, the property taxes will increase despite the quality of the academic institution.

The information in the pages that follow will explain how housing market value can be a gauge for public policy officials in determining how best to assist low-income communities in everything from education to economic stability. The circumstances in this text are not linear. Many outliers exist and can be mitigated in communities, and home prices can fluctuate for a variety of reasons, like natural disasters to predatory lending, yet the purpose of this narrative is to bring attention to a social concern and explain how public policy can help better aid low-income communities before these communities reach the state of decline. Social scientists, social activists, and even observations by Dr. Martin Luther King Jr. on his lodge on the West Side of Chicago tried to bring attention to community conditions and exploitation, but problems persist.

The Housing Market Value

Housing market value is a quantification for wealth because home value incurs equity. Equity is an economic asset that wealth is built upon because it accumulates over time.

Home value is a proxy for wealth because of its ability to create equity. Equity is generated interest that is afforded through property ownership. Equity, which generates and increases over time, becomes wealth. Equity as wealth is important because it can be transferred and passed down through generations. The housing market value is an additional component that allows real estate professionals and mortgage lenders to increase the price of a home because of public information, ethnic identity of neighborhoods, standardized test scores, or social amenities such as teacher salary and the academic character of a nearby school. Research by Feng and Lu (2013) explained:

When information relating to school quality is imperfect in the quasi-market for education, the disclosure of additional information can be utilized to identify the effects of school quality on housing prices if that information is exogenous to the housing market. (p. 291)

Consequently, housing prices instead of property taxes tend to be higher in communities in close proximity to institutes of higher education for reasons related to the university's culture and accessible college resources (Kashian & Rockwell, 2013; Vanegrift et al., 2012; Wen et al., 2018). To better illustrate, "undeveloped land has a significant negative effect on house price. A 10 percentage point increase in undeveloped land is associated with a 1.1 percent reduction in house prices" (Vanegrift et al., 2012, p. 323). Therefore, the value of a home, preferable to property taxes, is related to community factors and thus is under the authority of housing market professionals. Housing market value also includes public components of quality and achievement, which are computed using input and output variables.

Input variables are academic resources, which could include school scholastic assessments and classroom size, whereas output variables include test scores, student grade point averages, graduation rates, and continuous academic trajectory like higher education outcomes. Therefore, unsurprisingly, Vanegrift et al. (2012) revealed, "Results show that a one standard deviation increase in test scores results in housing prices that are between 1 percent and 14 percent higher" (p. 307). When these factors become public information, they are reported through school rankings or school report cards, and these elements are suitable factors in determining housing market value.

Imberman and Lovenheim (2016) stated, "Housing markets respond to the public release of school and teacher value-added information" (p. 105), which overarchingly makes community education less associated with property taxes and more affiliated with home prices. Educational reputation serves as a barometer for housing market value, as evidenced by the fact that home prices are higher in communities where academic institutions are performing up to standards, such as producing high test scores. Academic test scores alone are not a gauge for student success or even lifestyle outcome, but these scores are used for community marketing and social appeal. Information on this topic is generally available to the public and is explained in a variety of ways, but research by Feng and Lu (2013) reported that housing prices decline in regions that do not include prestigious schools, and Imberman and Lovenheim (2016) found, "A standard deviation difference in test scores is associated with a 2%-5% increase in the value of a home" (p. 104).

These housing elements describe the influence that home values have upon educational quality in a community. Academic quality is measured through academic status, qualifications of teachers and principals, and teacher-to-pupil ratios. The teacher-to-pupil ratio is a suitable gauge for educational quality because it relates to academic achievement. High-volume classrooms engender educational inequalities because of the large number of students per one teacher. Although academic merits are satisfactory barometers for school quality, the housing market also reflects variances based on racial compositions.

Community racial demographics influence market value home prices in some communities. Research provided by Kendi (2017) indicated that Black Americans have been linked to depreciating property values since 1793. A case study completed in Milwaukee, Wisconsin, determined that home prices in all-White communities gained an annual three percent value increase more than communities with minority constituents (Kim, 2000). Brasington et al. (2015) pointed out, "Houses in racially integrated areas sell for a discount compared to houses in more racially segregated areas. Increasing racial segregation by one standard deviation raises house prices by 3 percent, or $3,518" (p. 443). These price fluctuations have a pattern of changing with racial composition. A case study by Harris (1999) qualified the housing market value as a measurement of racial identity.

Harris (1999) stated:

> *Hedonic coefficients indicate that housing units lose about 16 percent of their value when neighborhood racial composition increases from less than 10 percent black to between 10 percent to 60 percent black. For the average dwelling, this is equivalent to a $1,187 reduction in annual cost. An even larger reduction in housing value is associated with moving from a neighborhood in which less than 10 percent of residents are black to one where at least 60 percent of the neighborhood is black. In this scenario, dwellings lose 46 percent of their annual value, which is equivalent to about a $3,351 reduction in annual housing cost for the average unit. (p. 471).*

The characteristics above are viewed as housing market values because home prices are significantly lower in predominately Black communities. A study from 2012 explained that "Blacks, on average, experience home equity growth that is nearly 17 percent lower than whites" (Loving et al., 2012, p. 441). In 2020, the *New York Times* reported that the homes of Black owners are assessed at lower values regardless of community wealth and despite the prestigious occupation and/or economic status that the person of color may obtain (Kamin, 2020). In some studies, home values increased by forty percent when the homeowner was assumed White.

Crime, Living Conditions, and Community Upkeep

A link between exploitation and disadvantaged people has existed for decades. Many of the same concerns that were addressed by the Kerner Commission (1967) are still valid today. The Kerner Commission was a multiple-case investigation of urban Black communities in the United States. The purpose was to probe northern Black cities for information related to the dissatisfied actions of Black Americans. The findings from this report were clear: Black Americans are socially, economically, psychologically, and politically antagonized. One example is that oftentimes when racial uprisings occur in communities, the stores that exploit the residents are violently targeted because of their monetary escapades. The events in Los Angeles in 1992 are clear examples of this notion.

Additionally, these communities can have limited resources, which are visible in everything from the type of businesses to the educational systems they sustain. However, being label or categorized as a low-income community doesn't necessarily mean that the individuals inside the community are all monetarily insecure, because those communities are serviced by immigrant businesses making large profits from the constituents.

Experienced scholars like Thomas Sowell (2014) have discussed this topic for decades and assert that businesses in disadvantaged communities are likely to be unprofitable because of crime (and theft, which cuts into profit margins); therefore, storeowners in these areas have to increase prices to make up for losses. Sowell's research has explained that these higher prices are not an example of cost exploitation but rather related to the cost of additional fees that exist in disadvantaged communities, such as insurance costs. Being experienced in a subject matter does not mean that perspective facts always fit the narratives of all groups involved, however. Eliminating overhead costs is a priority for all business owners, and it should be acknowledged that crime is a concern in some disadvantaged areas, but theft and/or robbery occurs in all communities, and shoplifting is not limited to a particular residential community. Also, law enforcement (in line with local politicians) chooses not to report crime in wealthier areas because crime is factored into community reputation (and property values). It is important to point out that thieves are more likely to shoplift outside of their disadvantaged communities because the quality of selections is potentially better.

Behavior and character are not indicative of the people inside of a community. One cannot assume that because a community is marketed as financially secure that monetary assets are associated with lifestyle. These do not correlate and are never linear. Above, I mentioned the unofficial case study of Dr. King in Chicago. In 1967, *Where Do We Go from Here: Chaos or Community* was published and explains the impact of poverty. Community poverty functions in a variety of ways that includes everything from the exploitation of financially insecure residents to limited transitions and life selections. King explained that this occurs because individuals with social limitations have fewer life selections and thus have to accept what is available. Thomas Sugrue's *The Origins of the Urban Crisis: War and Inequality in Postwar Detroit* (1996) investigated this notion and asserted that when disadvantaged people are spending more income than the affluent demographic on services, the result is that additional necessities like curb appeal in disadvantaged communities becomes a financial challenge. Thus, the imagery of the disadvantaged becomes defined as unattractive. These types of socioeconomic situations can lead to exploitation. Scholars over time have disagreed about the reasons why people who have less pay more, but in sum the latter argument is true in financially insecure communities.

Discussion questions

1. How does wealth define a community?
2. What are some social differences between financially secure and insecure communities?
3. How does the housing market value guide community economics?
4. When the housing market value is used as a barometer in a community, what are some outcomes and findings that can be correlated?

CHAPTER 2

Community Wealth

The research of Morton Grodzins (1958) explains that system movements occur in socioeconomic waves that result in a tipping point. Political scientists describe a threshold and/or a tipping point as traditional movements that occur because of corresponding feedback.

Tipping points can be racially driven, academically related, or have economic affiliation. For example, according to Grodzins (1958) and Rothstein (2014), racially segregated communities account for the tipping points of ethnic groups when viewed through the racial lens. Many community factors can be interrelated and, beginning in the 1970s, has been categorized as deindustrialization. Deindustrialization in its simplest form is the displacement of an industry, largely manufacturing. Although the outcome of industrial loss was starkly visible by the 1970s, in essence much of the decline began in the 1950s. Communities like Gary, Indiana, East St. Louis, Illinois, and Detroit, Michigan, are strong cases for how deindustrialization overlaps and causes tipping points.

These threshold movements can be seen in housing market values. The housing market value establishes a thread of regularity within a community in which several additional social sectors correspond with its system, like educational attainment and median household income. These types of movements can be described through the lens of *general systems theory*. General systems theory is an open-relationship model comprising an organism that corresponds to internal and external communication (Boulding, 1956; von Bertalanffy, 1969). A change in communication occurs when the system is suspended or responds to feedback that converts the order (Boulding, 1956). System movements occur in socioeconomic waves that result in demographic shifts. These movements occur because of corresponding feedback and become drivers in communities.

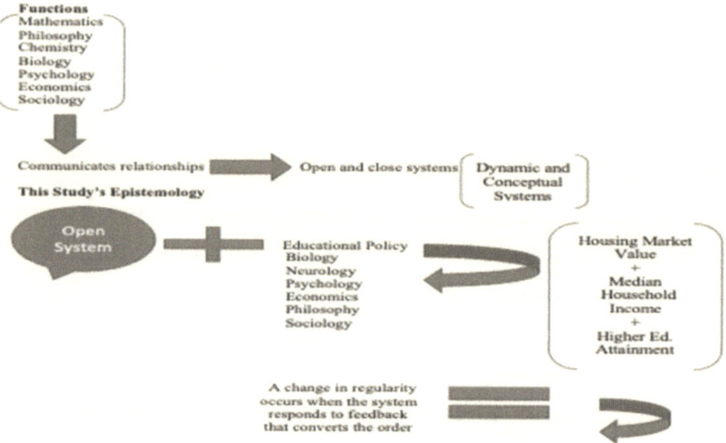

A variety of components can drive community wealth in the housing sector. A circumstance like deindustrialization is a correlation and can be an impossible feat to overcome unless industry repopulates the location. Correlation does not mean causation, and thus what this narrative is suggesting is that, upon economic tipping points, an intervention should take place to prevent an entire change in the community's environment. These thresholds are defined by using housing market values, because these values have been the most identifiable signals for the course of action in a changing community. Housing market values can change for a variety of reasons (as mentioned above), yet the outcomes of these change points have the ability to cause impediments in other areas of a community. This type of wealth flight can infect other social and economic sectors because these components comprise the population. Wealth flight is a change in a community's environment after the working class either moves or becomes the minority. Wealth flight functions much like capital flight. Capital flight is a shift in a nation's economic status in which the asset levels in a country changes (Cuddington, 1986; Leonce, 2016).

Capital flight transforms the economic hegemony of a country from vibrant to blighted (Chua, 2004). The causes of capital flight range from domestic economic choices to political strife or even crony capitalism, which is an interwoven system of country's politics that includes a dominant business sector (Chua, 2004). In situations where a country experiences a massive economic downturn like capital flight, foreign investors often contribute to the economic rebuilding process (Cuddington, 1986; Leonce, 2016).

The previous pages provided examples of housing assessments and how those values fluctuate upon different variables, and which ultimately change the wealth composition of a person and a community. However, additional factors contribute to the housing values of a community. Private owners (one person owns multiple properties) or real estate companies can purchase inexpensive properties in blighted communities and postpone renovation until after community reinvestment has occurred. This method contributes to a community's curb appeal. It is not sorcery that neighborhoods, communities, and towns supernaturally grow, develop, and change. These change points are methodical.

It is also important to understand that community grade is a function for banks determining recipients for business loans and/or beneficiaries for firm selections. This occurs because banks obtain revenue from loan interest and the ability to regain their investment. This is associated with resources because business owners establish firms in areas with the goal of gaining a financial return for themselves and the bank. Businesses and median household income (which will be discussed in Chapter 4) have a relationship because proprietors investigate the median household income in a geographical area via census data prior to establishing an enterprise. Examples of community transition can be seen in retail businesses. Retail businesses are also components of community wealth. Businesses in a community can account for household wealth because they contribute to geographical quality. This notion is illustrated geographically with stores like Whole Foods Market, Inc. or the Dollar General Corporation.

Does Race Matter in Communities Today?

Before we can discuss race and community presence, it's important to first understand race and how it has divided people among those lines. Collectively, the human species, *Homo sapiens*, comprises the human race, and although racial identity is a social construct, this construct is also a social reality. Therefore, it explains movements and how racial movements respond to predictive actions. Phenotype and genotype are not related. DNA is the material of human genes. Some genes are more dominant and others recessive. Melanin is created by all humans because light does not create melanin, yet pigment does create non-melanated people; as such, Black people have the ability to produce albinos. People around the world share

DNA because individuals have a united gene, mitochondrial deoxyribonucleic acid (mtDNA). Mitochondrial DNA is exclusive to the female chromosome and associated with generational genotype. Despite sharing DNA, many people have a shared genetic makeup simply because of ethnic and cultural reproduction. Blight (2007) described this phenomenon in terms of proximity: "Sexual abuse of slave women by young white men on farms and plantations rarely happened in random attacks; it occurred as a result of white control over a black women's time, labor, movement, and body" (p. 55). Comparatively, the work of Baptist (2016) alluded that this kind of "white man's sexual playground" (p. 238) could be the real reason it took a Civil War to end slavery in the United States, because "more than 400,000 out of four million American slaves by 1860 were categorized as mulatto or other terminology to distinguish a person of some white parentage" (Blight, 2007, p. 18). Many of these documented cases have been traced through scientific investigations, but some were never documented, so the number is potentially higher.

It is the unique genetic code of a person that determines outward appearance. To identify with a skin color is a personal choice that has been developed over time. Hegemonic attitudes, religion, colonization, imperialism, and ultimately the doctrine of discovery placed superficial "value badges" upon human beings for political purposes in order to control and divide. Although we live in a multiracial world and individuals are diverse and inclusive, it's important to recognize why people identify with a color and why unwarranted provocations are assigned to them based on it.

The United States can date its separation of humans by phenotype to colonial Maryland and Virginia. Evidence of this occurred when Black and White servants under indentured contracts relieved themselves of their duties. Upon capture, the severity of the reprimand was based upon skin color in 1640. State by state, anti-miscegenation laws developed over time, first in Maryland in 1664 and later in Virginia in 1691. Phenotype-based punishments and anti-miscegenation laws set the United States on a course for individual separation. However, Bacon's Rebellion of 1676 was the single event that created a purpose for Whites. This colonial Virginia uprising occurred when both Black and White indentured servants united against a common (but not perfect) cause. The outcome of Bacon's Rebellion added value to "White," and thus this course of action gave legal benefits to some based on that classification and denied others who lacked it. The purpose of this separation was to prevent any further biracial alliances. It is important to grasp the historical sense of where racial categorization originates, because individuals are judged based upon it.

Communities today have racial lines. Behavior and characteristics are learned. Conduct doesn't have a skin color, but research still suggests that, after a community surpasses its tipping point, conscious White flight will occur. Specifically, Grodzins (1958) asserted that, for each community, there is a certain percentage of Black residents that will "tip" an area from being integrated into becoming majority Black. Therefore, Grodzins (1958) concluded that integration can occur, but the Black population has to remain below a certain number.

Most working-class communities include diverse populations ranging along income lines. These parallels become racialized after a community has reached its tipping point. After the tipping point has occurred, disinvestment occurs in a community, and it has a relationship with the housing market values. A disadvantaged community, or a low-income environment, has been defined as a region with a poverty rate of greater than twenty percent (HHS, 2018). Poverty thresholds are defined by family (household) size as it relates to earned income (U.S. Census, 2020). To clarify, the poverty threshold for one person is $12,760, but for a family of four it is $26,200 (U.S. Census, 2020). The research of Sharkey (2013) explained that roughly a third of Black children grew up in high poverty communities compared to only one percent of White children between 1985 and 2000.

The economic status of the community is also not a reflection of its residents. Despite economic status, approximately forty percent of Black Americans live in areas considered under-resourced, while only nine percent of White families share the same experience (Eligon & Gebeloff, 2016). Black Americans are ten times more likely to live in a concentration of poverty regardless of economic status (Austin, 2013; Badger, 2015; Jargowsky, 2015).

Because dependents are considered economic liabilities, the U.S. Department of Health and Human Services defined poverty within a family according to income and the number of dependents. Applying this definition in practice, a family of four with an annual earned income of $26,000 or less is considered below the poverty line (HHS, 2018). The Supplemental Nutrition Assistance Program (SNAP) is an institution that provides low-income families with financial assistance identical to the former Food Stamps Program (U.S. Department of Agriculture [USDA], 2014). SNAP beneficiaries are measured via the USDA. Data provided by the USDA (2014) revealed that of the 470,098 SNAP recipients, 36.8 percent were White and 26.6 percent were Black. These numbers suggest that White Americans are more underprivileged than Black Americans, yet the economic status of White Americans does not reflect their living conditions in most geographical locations. As seen in the city of St. Louis, Missouri, "29.5 percent of poor African Americans live in concentrated poverty. Among poor whites, just 1.6 percent do. Poor whites, in most major metropolitan areas, are spread out. Poor African Americans are not" (Badger, 2015, p. 1). Low-income White Americans are not positioned as a unit into localities based on their income. Comprehensive case studies that focus on concentrated poverty explain that White Americans in rural areas like the Appalachian region and the Indigenous population on reservations in places like Montana live in poverty due to their economic status.

Some White Americans in disadvantaged regions experienced a decline in skilled and unskilled industrial and/or manual labor and as a result became sustained in disadvantaged circumstances. Government programs have focused on retraining, monetary assistance, and higher education in Appalachia for decades, and some programs are successful, yet several are not. Research provided by Zeitz (2018) claimed the creation of the "War on Poverty" was specifically for Americans who lived in Appalachia. The work of Isenberg (2017) legitimizes this notion and it's valid in places where White people were the majority and relied on the manufacturing and production of one industry, like coal. Although some Black Americans have ties to Appalachia, the overall issue concerning that area is related to the fact that men and women in this region have significant skills, but the employment opportunities that require these assets have deteriorated. Thus, the workers only owned their labor, and consequently their skills became liabilities when industry relocated. Communities' change points, as they relate to ethnic or cultural demographics, include racial tipping points. According to Rothstein (2014),

"Neighborhoods that appear to be integrated are almost always those in transitions, either from White to mostly Black (like Ferguson, Missouri) or from Black to increasingly White (like St. Louis's gentrifying neighborhoods)" (p. 3). These types of flight patterns can be exacerbated by urban planners, real estate agents, and city housing authorities. Kneebone (2014) reported how this situation occurred in Ferguson, Missouri (a suburb of St. Louis), when segregated public housing was placed alongside its growing middle-class Black population and the unemployment rate increased from seven percent in 2000 to over thirteen percent in 2012. Soon, the unemployment numbers increased, and reports explained that "By the end of that period, roughly one in four residents lived below the federal poverty line ($23,492 for a family of four in 2012), and 44 percent fell below twice that level" (p. 2).

By 2008, the majority of Ferguson had a poverty rate of twenty percent (some areas over thirty percent), which is the threshold poverty rate that negatively affects residents. The consequences of living in low-income communities are not directed toward the people inside the community but more so the economic change points that occur as a result because "an increased poverty rate of one percentage point is associated with a tax per acre that is 3.8 percent lower" (Vanegrift et al., 2012, p. 330). Granted, these transitions can develop due to investments and disinvestments, but what is factual is that these changes do occur. A significant number of people from poverty-stricken circumstances progress unaffected. However, the next chapter will explain that cognitive limitations are higher when poverty is a variable, because oftentimes survival mode becomes a social and economic characteristic when stress cortisol levels are high.

Discussion questions

1. How was deindustrialization impactful to communities?
2. Is ethnicity a cause for community flight patterns in modern times?
3. What are causes for community racial demographic change?
4. Why would community change points be related to economic changes?

CHAPTER 3

The Neurology and Psychology of Poverty, Place, and Education

Neuroscientists and experts (Farah, 2018; Lipina, 2017; Shapoval, 2015) who study the psychology of poverty identify limited cognition as one of several consequences of living in a low-income environment. This type of research explains causal interference and the impact of poverty as a function that has the ability to rewire the brain because individuals are situated in a disquietude situation. This research argues that individuals of poverty are more susceptible to these risk factors, not that they are personal constants. In support of this, medical studies have indicated that underprivileged individuals often have higher levels of cortisol, which is the stress hormone associated with memory loss, thought sustainability, and brain capacity (Blair et al., 2015; Cohen et al., 2006; Haushofer et al., 2012). Neuroscientists and experts who measure brain complexities gauge capacities by scanning the hippocampus and frontal cortex using PET, SPECT, fMRI ERP, and quantitative EEG (qEEG) imaging. These measurements can gauge the thickness of the frontal cortex, blood flow, and cerebral and brain activity, which determines memory sustainability and neurocognitive system function.

Farah (2018) explained:

Given the importance of brain function for academic and occupation success and emotional well-being, which are themselves causally related to SES, this would create a vicious cycle: a family's poverty would causally affect the capacities needed for socioeconomic success in the next generation (p. 64).

High hormonal stress levels are not specific to only low-income communities. The day-to-day workload of an emergency room doctor or nurse can beg to differ, but these are academic studies, and thus the objection is related to education and how children who reside in high-poverty communities are impacted and what can be done to improve the education of the youth. Environmental factors can cause these differences in brain formation. Research provided by Jenson (2009) claimed that it is imperative that educators are cognizant of the nonacademic circumstances of their students, and then they should use this knowledge to drive their instruction, realizing that some students may have external distractions which can become academic hurdles. Structural family support is important, and because of this household resources are influential. Resources are not only monetary but more importantly include attention, encouragement, and guidance, which comes by way of parents, guardians, or caretakers. Adjacent resources like coaches, teachers, and after-school recreational centers are just as impactful for the youth in said circumstances.

The mental hurdles of poverty can be overcome, and even when poverty causes adverse side effects, it is possible to reprogram the brain with positive factors. Surroundings that affect the psyche do not have an ethnic category or racial makeup. Individuals in low-income communities experience similarities regardless of self-identification, and therefore the goal is to identify the causal interference and develop action founded upon the symptoms. Historically, similar studies have been performed, and upon those investigations, legal strategic plans have capitalized on those findings over the years.

Case studies, sociological investigations, and focus groups all have a long history of influencing public policy. Take for example the study that was performed by Myrdal and Bunche (1944) which provided the sociological confirmation for the 1954 *Brown v. Board of Education* court case, and psychologists Clark and Clark provided the psychological study used as evidence in the case. These case studies demonstrated outcomes and side effects. The social scientists were not arguing absolutes but rather interference and social damage caused by conditions. Thurgood Marshall's NAACP team used the Clarks' psychological research (famously known as the doll studies) to document the profound ways in which de jure segregation affects Black children. Swedish economist Gunnar Myrdal (1944) was selected in order to objectively assess racial relations in the American South. These two studies, although different in context, had indistinguishable findings. The Clarks' research also determined that some individuals in inferior conditions think less of themselves because of overt structural differences, imagery, and societal positioning (*Brown v. Board of Education of Topeka*, 1954).

Supreme Court Chief Justice Earl Warren's written decision in the groundbreaking *Brown v. Board of Education* case acknowledged the impact of racialization:

> *Segregation of white and colored children in public schools has a detrimental effect upon the colored children. The impact is greater when it has the sanction of the law, for the policy of separating the races is usually interpreted as denoting the*

> *inferiority of the Negro group. A sense of inferiority affects the motivation of a child to learn. Segregation with the sanction of law, therefore, tends to retard the educational and mental development of Negro children and to deprive them of some of the benefits they would receive in a racially integrated school system* (Brown v. Board of Education of Topeka, 1954, para. 13).

These findings were not accepted by all, and research provided by Day (2015) emphasizes that individuals who opposed the above findings accused the social scientists of being "members of communist front organizations, socialist, or wholly ignorant of the situation" (p. 558). The publication of the *Southern Manifesto* (*Declaration of Constitutional Principles*) pamphlet written by Southern politicians a year after the *Brown* decision demonstrates the individual temperament by those who opposed the decision. For instance, Day explained, "No school district in Alabama, Florida, Georgia, Louisiana, Mississippi, North and South Carolina, and Virginia moved toward compliance" (p. 152). The movie *Remember the Titans*, in which a high school in Virginia remained segregated until 1971, illustrates an example of this noncompliance. And Busing in Boston in the 1980s in an entirely different conversation. The *Brown II* case demonstrated the harsh efforts to prevent the initial court rulings. Chief Justice Warren also inferred that White children develop a psychological superiority complex because of preferential treatment. The position by the chief justice did not decide that Black children academically benefited from being placed adjacent to White children. Graduates of historically Black colleges and/or universities often have a contrasting psyche to what Supreme Court Justice Earl Warren suggested, and the film *Hidden Figures* provides overdue accolades to Black female geniuses who were profoundly educated in segregated Black schools. Warren's conclusions were that social conditions have the ability to impede both socially and psychologically, and as a result the goal was to prohibit it.

Alternative research has insinuated similar factors, but in provocative ways. Fordham and Ogbu (1986) asserted that Black academic challenges are due to "internal and external factors" (p. 201). For example, Black cultural attitudes toward academics are the result of stereotypically associating academic success with characteristics affiliated with Whites or being accused of acting white. The term "acting white" has evolved through history from people who are unfamiliar with the academic dominance of Black Americans. Leslie Fenwick (2023), in *Jim Crow's Pink Slip*, explains that Black children prior to integration were educated by Black teachers who mostly all held graduate degrees from high-ranking institutions from the North, like the University of Chicago, and it was not until integration that those educators were dismissed. Buck (2010) explained that the term "acting white" developed during a time when racial integration began occurring in U.S. schools for the first time. Many Black students experienced opposition similar to that encountered by the "Little Rock Nine"—nomenclature assigned to the first nine teenagers who enrolled in Little Rock High School in 1957, only to find they were forbidden (although their parents tax dollars fund it) to enter by proclamation of the Arkansas governor. Buck (2010) described this experience in terms of an unconscious assimilation process that developed into a ridiculous belief because Black children were the students crossing over into the all-White academic sphere and not vice versa.

Whether the issue is internal or external, the above-all concern is that the problem persists, and the goal is to seek methods of mediation. Myrdal (1944) and the Clarks' investigations were geared toward racial segregation, but a similar inquiry particularly probed by the Clarks can provide a significant amount of insight if preformed between disadvantaged White Americans in places like Appalachia in contrast to overtly wealthy White Wall Streeters and vice versa. Social complexities are psychocultural elements, and these kinds of components develop over time into character traits. Psychocultural elements are aspects associated with individual ethnic groups that come by way of social conditioning. Therefore, one can speculate that since racial makeup and overt social mistreatment provide a clear and defining outcome, so can an investigation that centers economic class.

Discussion questions

1. In what ways do low-income communities affect educational outcomes?
2. How have case studies in the past been able to progress the United States more fairly?
3. Can you identify ways in which people can be recognized as a resource?
4. When does a community signify signs of negative social reactants?

CHAPTER 4

Impact of Housing Wealth and Educational Outcomes

Chapter 1 discussed the definition of wealth and how it can function through communities as an asset. This chapter will further explain how and why the same wealth has a correlation between educational outcomes. The AACU (2014) and the NSCRC (2016) have determined that the completion rates of college graduates among Black students from low-income communities are lower at every level of higher education measurement. Individuals without postsecondary education are more likely to experience a variety of social prohibitions that forestall upward mobility, such as widespread unemployment, limited healthcare, Granted, some research has suggested that Black students gain degrees and yet still over-index in opportunities that do not reflect their matriculation. Regardless of the perspective viewpoints, Black students enter higher education at significant rates, but the aforementioned is a predicament without matriculation, and thus it is important to recognize the weight that the housing market value has on community social sectors.

According to Antonakakis et al. (2015), data provided by Fannie Mae's National Housing Survey (2018), and statistical housing indexes gathered by Pulsenomics (2018), economic trends are reflected within the real estate market. The market value in a particular geographical location can suggest unforeseen recessions and/or economic progressions in a region. The relationship between the housing market and educational quality is related, and according to Wen et al. (2018), "From the perspective of educational quality or accessibility, kindergarten, primary school, junior high school, senior high school, and university significantly affect housing prices" (p. 68). This impact was observed with the redistricting of Shaker Heights, a prestigious community near Cleveland, Ohio, and concluded that it resulted in the reduction of home prices by 9.9 percent, or $5,738 (Bogart & Cromwell, 2000). Education and property value have a historical pattern of manipulation because, for instance, Manis (2001) explained, "The property of white schools was valued at $97.84 per pupil compared with $20.22 per pupil for black schools" in the beginning of the twentieth century in Birmingham, Alabama (p. 28).

This type of disparity was also demonstrated in wage compensation when at one time the Birmingham "school system paid white teachers an average annual salary of $827 but only $393 for black teachers" (Manis, 2001, p. 28), but more importantly, the link between the housing market value and higher education completion rates of Black students leads one to suggest that pipeline education is affected by community change points, which come by way of monetary real estate measurements. This parallel does not suggest that all students from affluent communities receive better educations than those who don't have access to those resources, but this connection explains that correlational factors that contribute to the higher education outcomes of some students.

Research shows that most individuals from affluent environments earn bachelor's degrees by age twenty-five, yet only one in ten from disadvantaged conditions can obtain the same goal (Bailey & Dynarski, 2011). The link between housing market values and education has implications that connect to higher education outcome. Former U.S. Secretary of Education and former president of the University of North Carolina Margaret Spellings (2006) suggested that imbalances in college graduation rates, completion, and attendance are correlated with racial identity and economic status. Spellings as well as Bailey and Dynarski (2011) highlighted the disparity in bachelor's degrees earned by age twenty-five among White, Black, and Latino adults and also among socioeconomic groups, with Whites significantly more likely to earn the degree in their twenties.

The housing market value establishes a thread of regularity within a community in which several additional social sectors correspond with its system, like higher education attainment and median household income. The information presented can be proxied for all ethnicities as it relates to the impact of the housing market values on higher educational outcomes. The issue presented was geared toward housing values in low-income communities, because what has been constant throughout this book is the issue that economic status does not always relate to living arrangements, because research has determined that Black Americans live in higher poverty regardless of their income status.

Poverty in the School System

In Pre-K-12 schools, the rate of poverty is measured by the number of students who qualify for free or reduced lunch (National Student Clearinghouse Research Center [NSCRC], 2016). If a school has a student population of fifty percent or more that qualifies for free or reduced lunch, then that school would be considered an under-resourced educational institution (NSCRC, 2016). Under-resourced schools gain a Title I rating and consequently receive monetary assistance from the federal government. Title I is a section of the Elementary and Secondary Education Act. Beginning in 1965, this piece of legislation provided monetary aid to schools with high poverty rates in efforts to support disadvantaged districts. These funds have been accessible for more than sixty years, yet excessive academic challenges continue to occur within under-resourced schools. For example, in Chapter 1, East St. Louis, Illinois, is introduced to demonstrate that the perspective of property taxes being the linear cause of community stability should be downgraded. Property taxes are an area of importance, but too many scholars incorrectly argue that when affluent households relocate from communities, consequently the tax base will decline the school systems. East St. Louis (District 189) has the highest property taxes in its surroundings, yet it has, in perspective, some of the largest academic challenges in its vicinity, despite receiving state and federal education revenue well over the state and national average (Crouch, 2011; Landis, 2017; NCES, 2019).

Historical accounts of resource discrimination in the education sector have been well documented over time. Researchers explain that in the past, in some states for example, districts received $14.75 per Black pupil and $49.37 per White pupil, and "white teachers averaged thirty-six students in their classes compared with fifty-eight for black teachers" (Manis, 2001, p. 28). These types of discrepancies are considered educational challenges and unequal resource allocations that have a pattern of affecting academic outcomes. Today, schools receive state and federal funds, yet impactful academic problems still exist. Education is a variable of property taxes, but higher property taxes do not always have a relationship to school quality or community sustainability. Academic contributions developed after studying communities like East St. Louis because, on average, low-income Black students attend under-resourced schools (Title I schools), and they are often not well prepared for higher education.

The median household income quantitatively summarizes the income in a particular location (i.e., Title I rating). To illustrate, in Chapter 2, I mentioned the underlining scope of banks and businesses and how they can cause some social environments to appear more attractive than others. Community poverty should not be mistaken for income circulating inside of a community. Low income should be viewed through the lens of the overall housing market value and the household income of some (not all) of the community constituents, because businesses survive due to the monetary exchanges of goods and services of patron traffic. Immigrants, like Koreans or Middle Easterners, consciously select these areas to service, and whether this is for exploitation or ministration, these businesses have to gain a profit in order to remain operating. Therefore, their mere existence is evidence of financial success. Hence, these communities have gains, but those advantages are not demonstrated in all areas of the social environment, such as the community school district as a whole. Economic imbalances that do not impact the school system segue into other components of academia, chiefly higher education. Organizations like the National Student Clearinghouse Research Center (2016) reported that eighteen percent of students from high-poverty high schools complete postsecondary education compared to fifty-two percent of students from low-poverty communities (NSCRC, 2016). Forty-eight percent of students from a low-minority high school obtained a higher education degree in six years; however, twenty-eight percent of students from a high-minority high school completed a degree in six years (NSCRC, 2016).

Four-Year Institution Graduation Statistics for Postsecondary Education in 2010

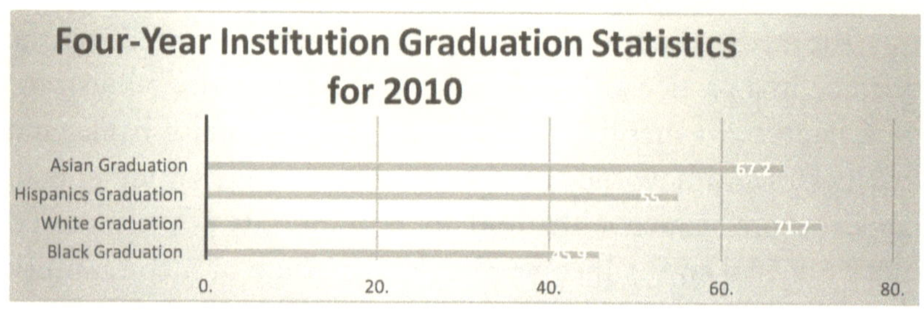

Note: Statistics derived from *Completing College—National by Race and Ethnicity—2017* by National Student Clearinghouse Research Center, 2017. Copyright 2020 by National Student Clearinghouse.

The NSCRC (2017) asserted that 62.4 percent of students who began attending a four-year institution in 2010 finished within six years. Collectively, when beginning at a four-year institution in 2010, Black Americans had the lowest higher education completion rate at 45.9 percent in a six-year period (NSCRC, 2017; Pell Institute, 2016). Comparatively, completion rates for Hispanics, Asians, and Whites for the identical period measured at 55.0, 67.2, and 71.7 percent, respectively (NSCRC, 2017).

Nationally, 39.2 percent of students who began higher education at a two-year institution in 2010 finished in six years (NSCRC, 2017). Degree attainment for Asians and Whites who started at a two-year postsecondary institution in 2010 was 45.1 and 43.8 percent, respectively (NSCRC, 2017). The average number of Blacks and Hispanics who graduated within six years with a bachelor's degree after beginning at a two-year higher education institution in 2010 was, respectively, 25.8 and 33.0 percent (NSCRC, 2017). The lagging numbers for all demographic groups suggest the pipeline education beginning in the Pre-K-12 sector may be associated with the low graduation numbers across demographics. Studies over the years have suggested such claims, largely beginning with a *Nation At Risk: The Imperative for Educational Reform* (1983), and jarring assertions were also documented by former U.S. Secretary of Education Rod Paige in his book *The Black–White Achievement Gap* (2010). The aforementioned are narratives that some may describe as "blaming the teacher" theory.

Educators are similar to police officers. Both are public servants. There are some good teachers (which I have experienced) and there are some bad (which I have also experienced). Categorically blaming the educator does not solve the root concern. Data are valid, but so are invisible circumstances that prohibited educators from performing their careers effectively. Screenwriter Quinta Brunson clarified to the world how influential former educator Joyce Abbott was to students in Philadelphia. Circumstances of poverty are related to degree attainment. The term "circumstances" is a category of risk factors that includes everything from a child attending school without the proper nutrition to teachers being under-resourced and not being provided the aid to properly support students. Social scientists and policymakers cannot ignore data and, uncomfortable as it may be, today as opposed to the past research does show that out-of-field teachers and less-qualified educators are in schools with high populations of Black students. This could be due to high turnover rates in some Title I institutions.

Carver-Thomas and Darling-Hammond (2017) revealed that the teacher turnover rate in Title I schools is fifty percent higher than that of schools not considered low-income. In addition, the turnover rate for math and science educators in underprivileged communities is up to seventy percent (Carver-Thomas & Darling-Hammond, 2017). When vacancies for teachers are high, education leaders hire educators who have fewer academic credentials and experience. Traditionally, individuals receive a Pre-K-12 education within their community of residence, and when that community is experiencing disinvestment or change points, as a result, all social sectors respond.

Universities and Communities

A variety of policies have acknowledged the need for higher education outcome studies that include communities that succumb to disadvantaged circumstances. Besides, the research provided by Du Bois (1899/2014), the Clarks (1989), and Myrdal (1944) suggested generations ago the correlation between community and social progress. The work of these researchers culminated in legislation that would be known as "The Great Society." In 1964, President Lyndon B. Johnson established Great Society programs. A component of Johnson's program was the War on Poverty, which he created after witnessing disadvantaged White Americans in the Appalachian region. The purpose of this program was to combat social and economic disparities across the United States. Another avenue of the Great Society was Johnson's focus on higher education for additional disadvantaged individuals, resulting in the establishment of TRIO programs as an educational sector of the program. In his commencement speech at Howard University, Johnson (1965) stated:

> *Ability is stretched or stunted by the family that you live with, and the neighborhood you live in—by the school you go*

to and the poverty or the richness of your surroundings. It is the product of a hundred unseen forces playing upon the little infant, the child, and finally the man (p. 4).

Johnson's actions were an example of Katznelson's (2006) assertion: "Public policy is used to compensate members of a deprived group for prior losses and for gains unfairly achieved by others that resulted from prior governmental actions" (p. 149). Since the late nineteenth century, a host of public policy figures have been involved in the sustainability of Black Americans in higher education. Anderson (1988) listed the following:

President Garfield was a trustee of Hampton, President Roosevelt served for nine years as a trustee of Tuskegee, and William Taft became a trustee of Hampton while President of the United States and was, in 1925, president of Hampton's Board of Trustees (p. 272).

On the other hand, Johnson's TRIO programs included trying to eliminate educational forestallments that occur prior to higher education. TRIO, which initially accompanied the Higher Education Act of 1965, referred to the act's three initial programs: Upward Bound, Talent Search, and Student Support Services. The original Higher Education Act of 1965 created federal monetary accessibility for students seeking higher education. The goal of the TRIO programs was to aid low-income, first-generation, and minority students in successful higher education attainment. The TRIO programs have successfully transitioned many students into the postsecondary sphere since their conception in 1965. Despite the guidance from the TRIO programs, the higher education completion rate for Black students from low-income communities continues to alarm. The concern with these incompletion levels is that higher education is a predictor of a better quality of life. The higher education success of students is predicated on the academic quality of their community. GEAR UP, Upward Bound, and Talent Search build partnerships between local communities and the higher education institutions in their respective areas. The programs focus on higher education curriculum adaptation, postsecondary transitioning, and financial aid availability.

In fifty-six years, the USDOE has been unsuccessful in reversing the social and economic forestallment that exists in higher education completion rates for Black Americans that come from low-income communities largely because the government-funded TRIO programs have limited student reachability due to service entry and funding. Some reports suggest that roughly ten percent of students have access to the programs, which culminates in the organization having a thirty-seven percent bachelor's degree completion rate for students on a six-year student track (Pell Institute, 2016). Government-funded Title I and Title II schools continue to face academic challenges that include everything from low standardized test scores to achievement gaps.

According to former Housing and Urban Development Secretary Ben Carson, "The role of the federal government is to facilitate the involvement of the state and local authorities in providing pathways that allow people to ascend out of poverty, not keep them in poverty" (as cited in Parker, 2017, p. 3). For these reasons, I assert that higher education policy and public legislation for postsecondary completion is more beneficial to all, regardless of ethnicity or economic status, when the focus is geared toward the community change points instead of individual student programs. These programs are important and should be sustained but be coupled with threshold rates, which come by way of the housing market value change points. By intervening upon community change points thusly, the entire area can benefit and produce better educational outcomes. Communities that habitually surpass their threshold, and by extension individuals who live in underprivileged conditions, are continuously filtered into less-privileged educational opportunities.

Challenges to Degree Attainment

Higher education researchers have explained that, of the several Pre-K-12 obstacles that hinder the higher education path and postsecondary sustainability for some students, the most significant prevention variable come from within the postsecondary sector (Aljohani, 2016; Boyraz et al., 2016; Spady, 1971; Tinto, 1975). Spady (1971) conveyed that higher education encompasses both an academic and social system. Both need to interlock at a satisfactory level to maintain student retention (Tinto, 1975). Collegians must keep satisfactory grades to maintain academic admittance, and thus a student's academic performance is a predictor for higher education completion.

The postsecondary environment has elements that intersect, and "when one views the college as a social system with its value and social structure, one can treat dropout from that social system in a manner analogous to that of suicide in the wider society" (Tinto, 1975, p. 91). Higher education administrators, faculty, and staff influence whether or not students remain enrolled and complete college. Several of these effects include students' postsecondary comfort and acceptance. To promote postsecondary retention, the American Association of State Colleges and Universities created an educational collaborative known as the National Retention Project. Comprised of 370 higher education institutions, its purpose is to assess student achievement in higher education by examining the entire institution rather than the individual student. Pamela Arrington, the former director of the National Retention Project, proposed that student acceptance, societal positioning, microaggressions, the socio-environment, and discriminatory comments create psychosocial conditions that force students out of higher education institutions (Townsend, 1994). Research indicates that all students need more mentors, and statistics reflect that the chances of a young adult not obtaining a college degree is more than seventy percent if their guardian did not graduate from college (Davidson, 2015, p. 6). Yet, even with this information, some facts tilt toward complications that partially occur inside the college. Mentorship influences student retention, but all cannot be allotted to an absent academic consultant. And a significant amount of research explains that although the internal environment can be good all the while, the external environment may be toxic and cause academic complications.

Environmental toxins are hazardous to individuals who live within the vicinity of the chemicals. Waste sites and chemicals like lead are harmful to an individual's health, resulting in educational setbacks for exposed individuals. Mohai and Saha (2015) used a longitudinal distance-based method to study 319 waste sites from 1966 to 1995 and determined that more than half of the minority population was likely to live near toxic sites. All levels of toxins are harmful, and their impact on the academic trajectory of those exposed becomes a challenge. According to a study performed by McKenna and Lavelle (2017), more than one million Black Americans are residents in communities that are home to chemical industries. Exposure to lead and other neurotoxins and/or chemicals occurs because these compounds are ingredients in a range of products such as paint, housing infrastructure, and pipes. Black children have the highest lead levels of all demographic groups (Bushrow-Cassidy et al., 2017; Levin et al., 2008). The CDC statistics from 1999-2002 revealed that 46.8 percent of Black children had lead levels higher than 5ug/dL (Levin et al., 2008). Blood lead levels are measured via microgram quantity (ug/dL), which is explained per blood deciliter. Some researchers link this ratio to economic status because lead levels in children from underprivileged communities are higher (Moody et al., 2016; Sampson & Winter, 2016). Flint, Michigan, is an example of modern lead poisoning due to its contaminated water source, which prompted the CDC to issue a public statement that there is no safe level of lead to ingest, and lead intake is irreversible. Furthermore, pregnant women exposed to lead transfer it to their unborn children. Lead has been linked to lower IQ scores, but having exposure to lead does not make a person IQ-compromised, and IQs have been known to fluctuate when an incentive is involved.

Intelligence quotient has been used over the years to prove scientific racism. Individuals who serve as professors, medical doctors, (Black women regardless of economic status still have the highest infant mortality rate of any ethnic groups) and the like are the culprits of this misinformation. Studies in books like *The Bell Curve* have been used to delegate untruths about Black Americans. Information as such can cause harm to Black children if believed, and the adults who write this information hide behind the First Amendment without taking into account other additional scholarship. Chiefly, the analyses of longitudinal data from a series of nine IQ tests administered to almost 15,000 children who participated in the Twins Early Development Study (TEDS) from ages two to sixteen years revealed a six-point IQ disparity between children from underprivileged conditions and privileged status before kindergarten (von Stumm & Plomin, 2015). By high school, the gap grew to a double-digit difference (von Stumm & Plomin, 2015).

Everyone comes from Africa but Scientific racist particulars are also detailed in *Mankind Quarterly*, which when analyzed argues that the same individuals who came (migrated) from caves (cavemen) are smarter than everyone by nature. *The New England Journal of Medicine* has also fallen victim to publishing disinformation about Black Americans. Needless to say, if IQ was attached to skin color, it would vary with skin tone. Black people produce albinos and all other phenotypes which has been proven by science, and those offspring do not have higher IQs because their skin tone is lighter. Phenotype (melanin level) does not determine the IQ capacity of a person. Blacks, Whites, and Asians all have different levels of melanin. These studies are false, and it's a good thing that Black children like spelling bee champion Zaila Avant-garde does not allow this type of information to impede her abilities.

Discussion Questions

1. Does wealth impact the higher educational rate of some students? If so, how?
2. What are reasons for poverty in communities?
3. How are property and housing market values related to education quality?
4. In what way is there a connection between median household income and education?
5. How are colleges and universities responsible for the retention of students?

CHAPTER 5

Applying What We Know and
Why the Tipping Point Matters

Education is the vehicle that gives an individual an opportunity to socially progress. Not getting a postsecondary degree can continue the repetition of disadvantaged circumstances. This research can enhance the existing scholarship in higher education leadership and strengthen educational policy that describes methods for increasing the low-income Black higher education completion rate.

Grodzins (1958) described the tipping point as a systematic shift in the social positioning of a community. Although Grodzins (1958) defined the tipping point of a community as a change in racial identity, this work suggests measuring the entire community's economic state by way of housing market values and median household incomes in order to disrupt and mediate further decline before it can permeate into additional social sectors. This strategy can be initiated by implementing social and economic structures to aid the community once it has been measured for trending toward a risky threshold tier. This can be done by implementing a steward of place upon tipping point ratios.

Monica D. Shepherd, Ph.D.

"Steward of place" is a term used to describe a regional higher education institution engaged in a collaborative relationship with its surrounding community (Association of American Colleges and Universities [AACU], 2012; American Association of State Colleges and Universities [AASCU], 2014). As stewards of place, many institutions around the United States have mutually beneficial relationships with their communities. The goal of a steward of place is to establish a thread of economic and educational influence in a community for enhancing the socioeconomic development of the region. According to the AASCU (2015), "68.5 percent of the AASCU campuses referenced their region in their mission statement, and all mentioned they had integrated community engagement into some aspect of strategic planning" (p. 7). The concept of being a steward of place is central to many institutions' missions and identities, yet opportunity gaps remain in many communities where economic and educational development are concerned.

The American Democracy Project, an arm of the AASCU, works to promote higher education civic engagement in local communities. The Carnegie Foundation has a similar goal. One of the more notable efforts in building a concrete concept of civic and community engagement came out of the Carnegie Foundation for the Advancement of Teaching, which in 2006 created a new voluntary classification scheme that highlights the work of campuses committed to partnerships with their communities. Subsequent rounds in 2008 and 2010 followed the 2006 Community Engagement Classification application and selection process.

Despite these and other efforts by higher education institutions to support their local communities, problems in many of those communities persist. Although college enrollment and completion rates increased in the 1970s and 1980s for

Black Americans (Ashkenas et al., 2017; St. John et al., 2013), Black college completion rates declined in the 1990s (St. John et al., 2013). Some researchers suggest that financial arrangements and college preparation are among the causes for the deterioration. For those reasons, educational policymakers have focused on higher education completion for people of color, first-generation students, and low-income students since 1965. Because education is viewed as the singular vehicle for overcoming generational poverty, the USDOE has increased the number of TRIO programs from three to eight. Despite the educational policy focus, higher education completion for Black students from low-income communities continues to be a challenge for university leaders and educational policymakers.

Individuals who do not complete postsecondary education increase their likelihood of experiencing various social phenomena that negatively impact their upward mobility. Completion increases one's chances of social improvement. As delineated in great detail throughout this text, consequently, since 1965, educational policymakers have maintained a focus on attainment of postsecondary education for students of color, students from low-income communities, and first-generation students, due to the fact education is perceived as a means to overcome generational poverty. Despite this focus and the increase of programs throughout the decades, higher education completion for Black students from low-income communities remains a challenge.

General Systems Theory Applied to the Tipping Point

In Chapter 2, general systems theory describes the dynamics of reactants and respondents. General systems theory operates by communicating relationship elements like open and closed systems, as well as dynamic and conceptual systems. An open system exchanges communication with its surroundings and thus evolves due to those external components (Luhmann & Gilgen, 2012). A closed system abstains from communication with external forces and consequently does not change (Bashiri et al., 2018). Mearman (2006) explained, "Closed systems are variously defined as being cut off from external influences, isolated where outside factors are neutralized, and in which all disturbances are anticipated and held at bay" (p. 46).

Dynamic systems theory is the explanation of how society, lifestyles, biology, and/or civilization divergences become identity differences (Fausto-Sterling, 2003). Conceptual systems are a confluence of perceptions that encompasses intersections of cognitive science and mental models (Lakoff & Johnson, 1980; Wallis & Valentinov, 2016). General systems theory is a useful model to use when describing empirical analysis because "it studies all thinkable relationships abstracted from any concrete situation or body of empirical knowledge" (Boulding, 1956, p. 197).

Since housing market values establish community direction as a result, any disruption of this system will redirect the overall system. The tipping point occurs due to change points rearranging the system. This information is consistent with the historical knowledge that is known about community turnover. One cannot ignore the historical patterns that have transitioned many communities over time. Although the focus is on how to benefit the present, in essence it is always beneficial to study the past in order to solve modern problems.

The Tipping Point and Race: Why is Race Still a Factor Today?

Historically, legalized residential segregation occurred as a result of President Franklin D. Roosevelt's New Deal (Katznelson,

2014). From that point forward, integration has been a complicated feat. Some community issues are related to income, and others not so much, but what is known is that communities change due to variables, and uncomfortable as it is, race is still one of those functions that is a part of community conversions.

Columbia University professor and urban history scholar Jackson (1985) stated:

> *The result, if not the intention, of the Public Housing Program of the United States was to segregate the races, to concentrate the disadvantaged in inner cities, and to reinforce the image of suburbia as a place of refuge for the problems of race, crime, and poverty* (p. 219).

This federal phenomenon established compound interest, equity, generational assets, and ultimately wealth for some Americans. These homes were further backed by insurance policies (like the Federal National Mortgage Association/Fannie Mae) that granted home loans exclusively to Whites who sought homeownership in all-White communities with restrictive covenants. Restrictive covenants (housing agreements) are a Northern version of the Jim Crow laws that saturated the South. In essence, all-White communities used restrictive covenants as a private racial bar for homeownership. The regulation, written into a deed of a home, prohibited non-White home seekers from moving into newly emerging suburbs. Additionally, veterans received monetary housing subsidies via the GI Bill, and those housing benefits included the same racial terms and conditions. To illustrate, the federal government provided thirty-year home loans with low interest rates, subsidized mortgage loans, and no down payments, which culminated in establishing the homogeneous suburb (Fishback et al., 2013; Katznelson, 2006).

Katznelson (2006) contended, "These loans were especially important in areas of high growth. In California for example, the federal government only had insured 6 percent of home mortgages in 1936; by 1950, fully half" (p. 115).

Besides restrictive covenants, redlining (the colorization of city maps to illustrate community quality) created racial division. Green represented superior residential locations, and red symbolized the lowest standards of property. First established by the Homeowners' Loan Corporation, the FHA later progressed this community rating system. Legal policies enforcing racial segregation, such as restrictive covenants and redlining, resulted in the manifestation of White flight throughout the United States. White flight is the voluntary relocation of White individuals from communities or schools. This transitional pattern has been significantly studied over the years and is insulting and overly used as a veneer for all community economic problems, as if White people are the only Americans with financial stability and thus have the resources to relocate today.

Presently, White flight encompasses Black Americans moving to the suburbs and White Americans relocating to further outer-ring suburban environments and/or adjacent homogeneous suburbs (Kye, 2018; Rothstein, 2014). This type of movement explains research provided by William Frey of the Brookings Institute (2018), in which he described the suburban environment as an enclave of racial diversity. However, upon deeper examination, neighborhoods in the suburb may be quasi-racially diverse, but diversity does not relate to equity and/or class status, because poverty and segregation in suburban environments continue to increase. Although legal measures discontinued restrictive covenants (*Corrigan v. Buckley*, 1926, *Hansberry v. Lee*, 1940, and *Shelley v. Kraemer*, 1948), empirical research by Kucheva and Sander (2014) supported the concepts of blockbusting and racial steering soon transpired as a phenomenon in most U.S. cities, despite the fact that residential housing discrimination became illegal in 1948. Blockbusting is the action of transitioning an entire street, community, or neighborhood into a majority Black demographic after the residency of a Black American. In many cases, real estate professionals were responsible for the covert violence against Black homeowners after purchases were made in all-White areas. This action was a phenomenon because the presence of Black residents in a community was viewed as a devalued neighborhood and extended and/or turned areas into redlined districts. This led to racial steering, which is the intentional practice of steering individual ethnic groups toward one community and, in turn, steering other groups elsewhere.

In the United States, real estate professionals and bank lenders operationalize racial steering and unethical lending practices. In 2003, the NFHA (2017) determined that racial steering practices occurred at eighty-seven percent when both Black and White testers posed as homebuyers. As proof, the NFHA (2017) organized a twelve-month tester study in which both Black and White homebuyers with the same credentials sought properties via a local real estate company in Jackson, Mississippi. NFHA (2017) researchers determined the "agents steered the White home seekers away from interracial neighborhoods in Jackson, which is majority Black, and into majority White areas such as Pearl, Ridgeland, Richland, Clinton, Madison County, Rankin County, and Pelahatchie" (p. 19). Testers are undercover investigators used by policy agencies to gather data in areas where disparities are deemed racially motivated.

Wells Fargo is the largest residential lender of home loans in the United States and was ordered to pay $7.5 million to the city of Baltimore and $2.5 million to several hundred of the city's residents for its discriminatory housing practices. Similar lawsuits have been filed in places like Oakland, California, where, according to the Bay Area News Group (2015), the attorney representing Oakland conveyed, "Wells Fargo's discriminatory conduct devastated individuals and communities, increasing poverty and wiping out or drastically reducing wealth from minority communities while bankers prospered" (p. 1).

Massey and Denton (1993) asserted that residential and education integration will be a perpetual challenge because of America's historical past of de jure residential segregation, which has become a de facto residential pattern. A significant amount of people believe that the problem is de facto related, but a study commissioned by the NFHA (2017) concluded that racial steering practices are the cause of modern community demographic compositions. According to the National Fair Housing Alliance (2017), there were 28,181 housing discrimination accusations in the United States in 2016. The report also determined that half of Black Americans do not live in a neighborhood with a White person, but on average White Americans live in communities that are eighty percent homogeneously White (NFHA, 2017).

A variety of academic institutions have attempted to measure racial bias by developing computerized examinations to implicitly identify personal prejudices. Those tests are problematic because a knowing person will answer opposite of their actual racial beliefs. "Racial bias" as a compound phrase is a euphemism. Either a person is racist or not. This notion can be argued from a variety of perspectives, but if a person is treated differently because of their skin color, that is a racial act and ultimately has been considered discrimination since 1964. Bias is a term that should be used to descriptively explain passive ideas. It should never be used to determine a person's overt actions toward another person because of their skin color. According to the U.S. Department of Justice (2020), computerized examinations do not have scientific value, and examples of their relevance are the reason polygraph tests are usually never used in court.

Public policy institutions have used testers for decades to investigate racial and sex discrimination in housing and schools, and the results determine that personal attitudes, and in turn race-based behavior, are causation for real estate steering patterns and some education disparities. In fact, former New York Senator and Secretary of State Hillary Clinton served as a tester in the South in 1972 to investigate all-White private schools and their willingness to desegregate after the *Alexander v. Holmes County Board of Education* case in 1969, which aimed to progress the second *Brown* ruling. Academic integration will always be a struggle when communities are segregated, but even when that became palatable, the notion of sundown towns began to socially saturate. Many of these all-White suburbs remained so because they were also sundown towns and/or suburbs. Sundown towns were communities that disallowed the presence of a person of color after dark unless it was a domestic worker. These towns and suburbs were more common in the Midwest; Illinois had more than 450 sundown towns, yet Mississippi had roughly six (Loewen, 2018). For example, Bridgeport, a neighborhood in Chicago where the Dan Ryan Expressway use to divide ethnic groups and where a Black child, Lenard Clark was nearly beat to death by local Whites for being in the "white neighborhood" in 1997. In essence, statistics like this give solid meaning to the popular phrase often spoken during the Civil Rights Movement in the North:. "In the South, the white man doesn't care how close you get, as long as you don't get too high. In the North, he doesn't care how high you get, as long as you don't get too close."

The Housing Act of 1949 and the Highway Act of 1956 both played roles in the methodical separation of Black and White Americans. The Housing Act of 1949 was an extension of the 1937 Public Housing Program, which created the housing project phenomenon in the United States. The federal government created housing projects with the intent to dismantle community slums. The objective was to grant low-income homes to the working underprivileged. Initially, public housing projects advocated strict policies that granted access to low-income nuclear families, but they did not permit single mothers or welfare recipients. Public housing projects were segregated by racial identity in most cities. Later, the Highway Act of 1956 socially and economically segregated individuals by race.

The routes of urban interstates were carefully chosen to disrupt Black neighborhoods and to erect physical barriers between minority and majority populations. Gary, Indiana, located its freeway to act as a Great Wall between its Black north side and the White south side. Atlanta did the same with I-20 and Orlando with I-4. In Miami, I-95 cleared African Americans from Overtown neighborhoods, adjacent to downtown, and pushed them farther away from the city center. In St. Paul, Minnesota, an urban interstate displaced one-seventh of the city's African American residents. One critic commented bitterly that very few blacks lived in Minnesota, but the road builders found them (Abbott, 2007, p. 86).

By the 1970s, Black poverty was systematically segregated into public housing projects, and White poverty received subsidized housing vouchers that positioned this demographic into mixed-income, multi-family units (Jan, 2017; Rothstein, 2017). Rothstein explained that Black Americans did not receive residency vouchers until 1998. To illustrate, in 1974:

> *A federal appeals court concluded that segregated housing in the St. Louis metropolitan area was . . . in large measure the result of deliberate racial discrimination in the housing*

market by the real estate industry and by agencies of the federal, state, and local government (Rothstein, 2014, p. 4).

The Fair Housing Act was signed one week after Dr. Martin Luther King Jr.'s assassination on April 11, 1968. Fair housing is one of America's best pieces of legislation, but limitations exist when public housing is incorporated into a community by racial classification and not economic status. Public housing is good, but it should be more aggressively arranged among all communities as mixed income. According to Perkins and Sampson (2015), middle- to upper-class Black constituents are residents in communities that are more disadvantaged than are low-income Whites, and research provided by the National Academy of Science determined that Black Americans, more than any other ethnic group, are more likely to live in a community with a poverty rate of forty percent or higher, despite economic classification (Firebaugh & Acciai, 2016). Today, Black Americans are wealthy, working-class professionals, and some are represented as disadvantaged, but what the above numbers suggest is that the Black class status is not always reflected in the community in which they reside. Although some of these statistics could be studied through the lens of income inequality, facts as such should be invalid in modern times.

Discussion Questions

1. How does a steward of place benefit communities that are trending toward economic decline?
2. What are some reasons for the declining graduation rate for enrolled college students?
3. How does general systems theory apply to communities?
4. Do historical housing patterns affect us today?

CHAPTER 6

Stewards of Place in Higher Education

Stewards of place are universities that partner with communities to focus on regional and academic reciprocity. These types of mergers provide social capital that benefits students seeking higher education. Higher education institutions serve as stewards of place because they establish a reciprocal relationship with regional communities through civic engagement, K-12 collaboration, economic development, and internationalization. Stewards of place establish a partnership with communities to build reciprocal outreach engagement. This union aims to provide economic, cultural, and social service programs that benefit both the region of influence and the postsecondary institution. A variety of these resources includes elements affiliated with the institution's higher education mission. This association is essential for constructing new and assessing old educational policy objectives because policymakers can evaluate this relationship and review constituency challenges and measure outcomes.

The Carnegie Foundation for the Advancement of Teaching is an academic network that has developed an educational strategy and leadership policy in the sphere of academia since 1905. This organization developed a variety of academic principles, including the Carnegie classification system in higher education. In 2002, the American Association of State Colleges and Universities produced an action plan for higher education institutions to become involved in regional academic policy and community economic enhancements. Comprising over 400 public colleges and universities, the AASCU has been in operation since 1951.

In 2005, the Carnegie Community Engagement Classification emerged to operationalize the ranking of postsecondary institutions that were in partnerships with their communities. The collaborative efforts of the Carnegie Community Engagement Classification and the American Association of State Colleges and Universities established stewards of place in 2006. Two years later, AASCU member campuses "accounted for just over 34 percent of institutions receiving this classification in 2008, and AASCU campuses made up over 28 percent of all classified campuses" (AASCU, 2014, p. 4). Today, higher education institutions that become stewards of place promote a diverse educational experience through the scope of academic leadership, federal and state public policy, and economic community advancement. A large portion of the programs that are established via a bridgeway provide attention to the Pre-K-16 pipeline, civic engagement, and higher education connectivity.

Stewards of Place and the Pre-K-12 Pipeline

Stewards of place include academic guidance and public policy relevance that pertain to students and faculty. Higher education institutions that act as stewards of place focus on curriculum standards, financial aid guidance, leadership training, preparatory coursework, and academic content that can be beneficial in the postsecondary sphere. Several of the subcategories include academic mentorship programs for students, elements of technology and distance learning, professional training, and certificate programs. As a transitional enterprise, stewards of place measure their academic and community engagement levels by quantifying partnerships post hoc, with site visits, and through student audits. Collected data can serve as indicators for determining the academic needs of students and faculty in the Pre-K-16 sector over time. This information can also provide insight that can contribute to the understanding of higher education disparities that exist between cohorts, ethnic groups, and contrasting income levels. The data can reveal the impact of college preparation courses and the significance of academic leadership mentors or higher education counselor services.

Higher Education Reinforcement and Community Economic Development

Higher education institutions that are stewards of place also collaborate with community investors in the public and private sector to assess regional challenges and seek ways to resolve microeconomic issues. The objective of this collaboration is to enhance economic sustainability in geographical locations that can benefit from regional guidance. The intent is to become both an economic and academic asset inside the community. The impact of these partnerships can result in everything from postsecondary institutions inhabiting physical spaces in communities to resource service opportunities and workforce development. The higher education and community exchange can attract both domestic and international organizations to a location by establishing goals, objectives, and strategic economic plans that align with enhancing community and regional infrastructure.

This engagement also includes global correspondence, internships, and academic outsourcing that aligns with postsecondary learning. These strategies establish successful partnerships with communities across the United States to enhance social and economic community deficiencies.

Town-Gown Collaborative

Town-gown relationships were an element of the Morrill Land Grant Act of 1862, the Land Grant Act of 1890, and most faith-based higher education institutions. In 1992, the U.S. federal government expanded its involvement in communities with the Community Outreach Partnership Center Program facilitated by the Department of Housing and Urban Development. HUD created the Office of University Partnerships (OUP) in 1994 with similar aims to provide monetary resources for universities that participate in town-gown partnerships. Cooper et al. (2014) reported, "In its first year, the OUP distributed $9.8 million to eighteen institutions in ten states across the country to support the creation of Community Outreach Partnership Center (COPC)" (p. 89). COPC and other modern town-gown partnerships were the proposed solution for deindustrialization that occurred in many regions of the United States. These partnerships revitalized several cities that had experienced decline due to revenue collapse. Today, more than half of postsecondary institutions (roughly 2,000 schools) are situated in central cities, and because of that some suggest that university and community integration is a progressive leap for disadvantaged communities, but the collaborative also triggers gentrification.

Town-gown collaboratives are combined social and economic entities represented by a higher education institution and its host community. Examples of town-gown collaboratives are seen via most secondary organizations. Town-gown partnerships are similar to stewards of place because these coalitions bridge community and academic relations. The Coalition of Urban and Metropolitan Universities (2018) includes over ninety postsecondary institutions, and the Coalition of Urban Serving Universities (2018) encompasses thirty-seven urban research higher education institutions. Town-gown collaboratives are sizable economic examples of stewards of place.

Town-gown collaboratives create social and economic advancements that mutually benefit both the region and the institution (Coalition of Urban and Metropolitan Universities). These exchanges act under the supervision of university presidents and chancellors. The CUMU and the CUSU aim to stimulate economic growth in their communities and increase higher education completion for students who face social and economic challenges. These urban-serving universities establish public relations through a variety of community avenues, including Pre-K-12 institutions and the business sector, and in most cases these establishments serve as anchor institutions for economically deficient communities. Economically, anchor institutions can encompass anything from a public health facility to an automobile manufacturing enterprise. Academically, anchor institutions are higher education establishments because these operations create employment opportunities for the surrounding regions.

Town-gown partnerships engender economic growth on a large scale, which can independently stimulate substantial economic sectors such as medical centers, research institutions, Pre-K-16 academic centers, technology facilities, and a host of other sizable infrastructures. On the other hand, a college town is a community that has an anchor university and a dependent economic district, which typically consists of a vibrant downtown region supported by the institution.

College towns typically have an evolving young demographic and a high renter population, which establishes the community as a "student ghetto" (Massey et al., 2014, p. 156) that avails "studentification"(p. 156). Studentification is the process of having a large student population in a community and, accordingly, the local and social industries reflect that demographic. College town communities differ from town-gown partnerships because college towns often encompass an economic sector supported by the student population, while town-gown collaboratives consist of larger economic community relationships like infrastructure.

Discussion Questions

1. How do stewards of place benefit communities?
2. What is the impact of stewardship?
3. Are there liabilities to developing a steward of place in a community?
4. In what ways do town-gowns and stewards of place contrast?

CHAPTER 7

Model Application

The above pages lead to the perspective that the difference of location creates contrasting educational opportunities. The emphasis on opportunity is essential, since education is the initial vehicle that grants subsequent possibilities that carry into the higher education environment and affords opportunities after that. These circumstances can be measured by way of the housing market. Below is a particular model that can be used in a variety of communities to determine the change point at which household wealth negatively impacts the educational attainments of Black students:

1. A quantile regression (QR) model measures the percentile strength of the dependent variable to seek a quantile change point in household wealth and median household income, which stimulates a percentile change in postsecondary education attainment of low-income Black students. The QR is a prediction synthesis. The emphasis of relational strength is on the dependent variable rather than the covariant. Each variable should be measured every tenth quantile—that is, from the 10th through the 90th—to determine the stage of significance upon the dependent variable

from a low level of impact to a high level of influence. The predictor variables should be median household income and housing market values, which are proxies for wealth. The higher education completion measurement should be represented by the Y variable and serve as the response measure.

2. This QR model can be used to identify transitional time, strength, dates, and/or nonlinearity sequences along a distributional continuum. This QR model can include the bootstrapping method. This procedure is used to resample observations (n) at different time periods (e.g., 2000-2023) in order to estimate the mean of the random sample. The coefficients should be derived through bootstrapping (x_j) based on 10,000 replications. Bootstrapping is widely utilized in the field of statistics when the information is empirical.

3. The control variables should include the total population per year, the Black-to-White population ratio, retail trade establishments in the community, student-to-teacher ratios, and public education budget allocations per year in the city. These factors should also be measured from the 10th through the 90th quantile to determine the level of significance they have upon the dependent variable. The Black-to-White population ratio should be used to determine the movements of racial demographics during the years under examination. The total population affects resources because individuals move to school districts that have a better quality of education. Educational quality should be measured through the scope of student-to-teacher ratio because it represents the amount of attention allotted to each student.

The budget per student provides quantifications for monetary aid provided to a district. The public education budget allocation per year in the community illustrates the availability of academic resources per student, which has a relationship with educational quality. The number of active retail trade establishments in an area demonstrates available constituent capital in a community and, as a result, can serve as measurement for educational quality because community residents subsidize district schools. Use population movements, statistical patterns, and wealth change to pinpoint a quantile wealth threshold that a community can withstand before higher education stewardships are deemed necessary. D_t was a binary/dummy variable equal to one during the recession periods, as defined by the National Bureau of Economic Research (NBER), and otherwise zero.

As previously stated, the dependent variable of this study is HEA_B, while the primary independent variable is household wealth as proxied by ΔHP and ΔHPCI. A set of previously defined control variables, Z, which include POPN, WTBR, BIZ, STR, EDUBGT, and STR, are also included in the model. Formally, the traditional multiple regression equation based on the previously mentioned research variables is formulated as follows:

HEA_B =

$$\alpha_i + \rho_1 \Delta HP + \beta_1 POPN + \beta_2 WTBR + \beta_3 BIZ + \beta_4 EDUBGT + \beta_5 STR + \beta_6 D_t \qquad (1a)$$

HEA_B =

$$\alpha_i + \rho_2 HPCI + \beta_1 POPN + \beta_2 WTBR + \beta_3 BIZ + \beta_4 EDUBGT + \beta_5 STR + \beta_6 D_t \qquad (1b)$$

Unlike a multiple regression equation, which is premised on the conditional mean of coefficient estimates, quantile regression, proposed by Koenker and Bassett (1978), offers several benefits in econometric modeling. A QR model provides more in-depth analysis upon the dependent variable at different stages. This study used a QR model to identify the point at which a change in household wealth and median household income per capita trigger a percentile shift in postsecondary school education attainment of low-income Black students.

The QR model captures the entire regime relationship of the predictor variables and their influence on the response variable. This model is used to study the distributional relationship of the response variable at different quantiles, which measures the entire outcome dispersal. Quantile regression models generate rich dynamics and nonlinearities. Formally, one can base the QR on the variables below. It is modeled as follows:

$$\text{HEA\_B} (\tau \mid \Delta HP, D_t, Z) = a(\tau) + \rho(\tau)\Delta HP + \beta(\tau)Z_t \qquad (2a)$$

$$\text{HEA\_B} (\tau \mid \Delta HPCI, D_t, Z) = a(\tau) + \rho(\tau)\Delta HPCI + \beta(\tau)Z_t \qquad (2b)$$

The parameters in Eq. (2a) and (2b) are minimized, and thus the weighted of each τ are estimated from its absolute deviation. $\rho_\tau (u) = u(\tau - I(u < 0))$, $0 < \tau < 1$, and I is the indicator function. Eq (3) is a minimization problem that is solved from linear programming.

$$\tau \text{ as follows: } \underset{a(\tau) + \beta(\tau)}{\overset{arg\ min}{}} \Delta HPCI\rho_\tau(HEA\_B - a(\tau) - \rho(\tau)\Delta HP - \beta(\tau)z_t) \qquad (3)$$

Applications

These formulas are used for investigating the problem of persistently low college completion of Black students through the framework of government housing policies that shape economic stability and wealth. These policies have been established through federal and state government actions and are perpetuated through local real estate markets and practices. Therefore, the below implications are for higher education leaders to both develop new ways for institutions to be stewards of place and to focus on intra-institutional changes.

The implication for this study is that stewards of place can attempt to reverse community wealth downturns upon quantile thresholds in circumstances where geographical wealth declines and thus affect higher education outcomes. These steward models include creating a researcher position inside of higher education institutions. This position would be a liaison higher education role that would work with local and state departments of education. This relationship should also include an alliance between both the local and state boards of education.

Wealth affects higher education outcomes on time-varying occasions; state agencies should receive local school district data in order to develop threshold interventions. The state department of education has the authority to enact policies for public schools, state colleges, and public universities. State education policymakers should focus on disrupting the alarming signs of wealth decline by employing measures upon academic thresholds. The objective should be to intervene prior to grave educational impact. These interventions should focus on employing academic guidance in underperforming districts, since economic thresholds affect higher education attainment at time-varying stages. Stewards of place could be beneficial if implemented upon threshold rates since tipping points trigger additional downturns. Threshold interventions should focus on the declines and be geared toward sustained asset growth. A partnership among state colleges, universities, entrepreneurs, and regional business owners could help defend against economic downturns, which have proven to affect higher education attainment. Higher education institutions can partner with individuals in the business sector for the purpose of creating economic growth and investments.

This partnership can occur in two ways. First, this collaboration should occur on wealth thresholds and consist of creating a regional higher education campus in the disadvantaged community. This relationship has the potential to create both employment opportunities, which could increase the median household per capita income, and also prevent the depreciation of real estate prices, because both are proxies for wealth. Wen et al. (2018) explained, "From the perspective of educational quality or accessibility, kindergarten, primary school, junior high school, senior high school, and university significantly affect housing prices" (p. 68). Accordingly, both the median household per capita income and median housing values were the primary regressors for the varying change points in the previously performed studies.

Second, a regional higher education branch in a disadvantaged community could prevent time-varying economic changes that affect measures of education. Therefore, a college campus has the potential to develop additional economic sectors. Simultaneously, business owners can invest in infrastructure that may be experiencing a transitioning change point due to varying wealth shifts. Everything from restaurants to leisure activities can evolve because economic capacity, like a higher education institution, would create population necessity, and these social sectors create job opportunities. Occasions as such could increase median household per capita income if social sector employment opportunities were allocated to individuals from the community.

Discussion Questions

1. How does a quantile regression determine change points?
2. In what way is a quantile regression more actuate than a linear regression?
3. What is the benefit of knowing the change point in a quantile regression?
4. In what way do control variables impact this study?

Afterword

Analysis of these data indicate that researchers should understand the complex relationships between past policies, housing, wealth as an economic asset, and education trajectory in order to comprehend and act upon modern education leadership problems that involve Black Americans. It is important to acknowledge particularly the strength of the median housing value through the lens of general systems theory. A community's housing value is its nucleus. Additional social elements affect its residential stability and/or instability. Cases like these can be used to study Pre-K-12 quality, change points, and ultimately higher education attainment. Students in low-income communities often experience academia in underperforming schools, which can lead to later struggles within higher education. Wealth statistics can provide information that shapes state departments of education and federal policy for threshold interventions.

The mode presented used the housing market value and median household per capita income as regressors in order to seek the impact that wealth has on low-income, Black higher education attainment at different change points over time. These different distributions are also found in the control variables. These particular findings are interchangeable observations in other geographical locations. Community observations can vary depending on the economic and social landscape of the population. Some community variables have more of an impact on community movements, and those variables may influence a greater response upon the levels of education downturns, uptrends, scarcities, and higher education patterns than the factors observed in Chapter 7. Employment opportunities are pull factors for geographical locations. A deeper approach on this subject could suggest that employment selections are a stronger regressor for higher education outcome because they affect the residential patterns of the entire population. Further, higher education leaders are limited in their abilities to correct community education problems. State and federal policymakers can address several of the investigative concerns.

The purpose of this investigation was to bring attention to a variety of components that correlate to change points in communities and how those waves cause respondence in the social and economic spheres. The aim was to identify the reasons community reactance occurs and contribute to remedying the problems. My contribution to scholarship is recommending that knowing the quantile measure for the community and utilizing the proper model can in turn grant higher education leaders the ability to influence students in geographical locations that are potentially prone to the effect of community educational downturns. Education begins early, and therefore the goal of this information is to benefit communities that may have experienced time-varying positive effect of household wealth on the higher education attainment rate of low-income Black students.

Empirical research suggests that access to privileged locations affects educational trajectory. Granted, location and affluence are not the only predictor variables for academic trajectory, because some individuals who have access to privilege fail to progress and struggle with attempts to do so. The influence of peers and guardians has the ability to impact progress regardless of location, but privileged locations can greatly influence progression in the educational sector. Time-varying movement does not apply to all communities, and in no way do low housing prices mean that the community is always Black residents. Black is never a synonym for poverty or any other adjective/euphemism that means financially unstable. This research is not wholly about that. Therefore, what this information set out to do was to formulate a parallel in order to assist communities that have been struck by waves of socioeconomic change.

This research explained that a satisfactory community threshold that equates to resource accessibility can be a remedy to disrupting higher education impediments for some. Therefore, this information serves as a guide to alleviate the problem. Pipeline education is important, but so are factors inside the higher educational sphere. Home life and social environments also are components of a successful educational trajectory. Many have forgotten that schools used to be safe spaces. For some, the academic institution was a refuge from external ills. Schools functioned as a place of hope for those that did not experience it anywhere else. The change in communities is in essence a change in schools. A popular critique from older generations who experienced segregated Black schools is that the school was the community. The United States has never tried separate but equal. In the past, it had always been separate and unequal. Black institutions have historically been underfunded intentionally, and those schools during the Jim Crow era still produced some of the best American minds. Today, schools get a significant amount of funding, and thus additional problems arose as society changed and communities began to be saturated with toxins that often set the stage for common urban circumstances.

American author and Detroit native Donald Goines is the best writer on the topic of urban life, resources, and survival. His book, *Black Girl Lost* (1973), is fiction, but the story is real.

The lead character, Sandra, is a brilliant reader with a genius-level IQ, but she doesn't attend school because her attire (and overall home life) is disappointing, which affects her self-esteem. This jarring portrayal by Goines allowed for academic research and fiction to fuse. Although there have been focus groups, surveys and overall academic probing about the emotional well-being of contemporaries, peers, and adolescence at school in turn, the story by Goines is a better feat. Because when a student doesn't attend school for social reasons, that child, although smart and capable overall, is labelled a dropout without anything else being considered. They will never matriculate in order to reach their potential and they are labeled incapable when in all actuality the former was never the problem. The circumstances of cause and effect are real, and unless individuals begin to give weight to that argument, there will always be a sector of society that will continue to blame the victim.

Bibliography

Abbott, C. *Urban America in the modern age, 1920 to the present.* Library of Congress, 2007.

Aljohani, O. A. "A Comprehensive Review of the Major Studies and Theoretical Models of Student Retention in Higher Education." *Higher Education Studies, 6(2),* (2016): 1-18. https://doi.org/10.5539/HES.V6N2P1.

American Association of State College and Universities. "Stepping Forward as Stewards of Place." (2002)

American Association of State Colleges and Universities. *Becoming a Steward of Place: Lessons from AASCU Carnegie Community Engagement Applications.* (2014)

American Association of State Colleges and Universities. "Operationalizing Stewards of Place: Implementing Regional Engagement and Economic Development Strategies. (2015)

Anderson, J. D. *The Education of Blacks in the South, 1860-1935.* University of North Carolina, 1988.

Antonakakis, N., Gupta, R., and Andre, C. "Dynamic co-movements between economic policy and housing market returns." *The Journal of Real Estate Portfolio Management, 21(1),* (2015): 53-60. https://doi.org/10.1080/10835547.2015.12089971.

Ashkenas, J., Haeyoun, P., and Pearce, A. "Even with Affirmative Action, Blacks and Hispanics Are More Underrepresented at Top Colleges Than 35 Years Ago." *New York Times*

Magazine (August 24, 2017). https://www.nytimes.com/interactive/2017/08/24/us/affirmative-action.html.

Austin, A. "African Americans are still concentrated in neighborhoods with high poverty and still lack full access to decent housing." Economic Policy Institute, 2013. https://www.epi.org/publication/african-americans-concentrated-neighborhoods/.

Badger, E. "Black Poverty Differs from White Poverty." *Washington Post*, August 12, 2015. https://www.washingtonpost.com/news/wonk/wp/2015/08/12/black-poverty-differs-from-white-poverty/.

Bailey, M., and Dynarski, S. "Inequality in Postsecondary Attainment." *Whither opportunity? Rising inequality, schools, and children's life chances*, edited by G. J. Duncan and R. J. Murnane, 117- 132. Russell Sage Foundation, 2011.

Baptist, E. E. *The Half Has Never Been Told: Slavery and the Making of American Capitalism*. Basic Books, 2016.

Bashiri, T., Vaezpour S. M., and Nieto, J. T. "Approximating Solution of Fabrizio-Caputo Volterra's Model for Population Growth in a Closed System by Homotropy Analysis Method." *Journal of Function Spaces* (2018): 1-10. https://doi.org/10.1155/2018/3152502.

Bay Area News Group. "Oakland Sues Wells Fargo for Predatory Lending to City's Black, Hispanic Residents." September 22, 2015. https://www.eastbaytimes.com/2015/09/22/oakland-sues-wells-fargo-for-predatory-lending-against-citys-black-hispanic-residents/.

Blair, C., Berry, D., Mills-Koonce, R., and Granger, D. "Cumulative effects of early poverty on cortisol in young children: Moderation by autonomic nervous system activity." *Psychoneuroendocrinology, 38*(11), (2013): 2666-2675. https://doi.org/10.1016/j.psyneuen.2013.06.025.

Blight, D. W. *A Slave No More: Two Men Who Escaped to Freedom, Including Their Own Narratives of Emancipation.* Harcourt, 2017.

Bogart, W. T., and Cromwell, B. A. "How Much is a Neighborhood School Worth?" *Journal of Urban Economics, 47*(2), (2000): 280-305. https://doi.org/10.1006/juec.1999.2142.

Boulding, K. E. "General Systems Theory: The Skeleton of Science." *Management Science, 2*(3), (1956): 197-208. https://www.jstor.org/stable/2627132.

Boyraz, G., Horne, S. G., Owens, A. C., and Armstrong, A. P. "Depressive Symptomatology and College Persistence Among African American College Students." *The Journal of General Psychology, 143*(2), (2016): 144-160. https://doi.org/10.1080/00221309.2016.1163251.

Brasington, D. M. "Which Measures of School Quality Does the Housing Market Value?" *The Journal of Real Estate Research, 18*(3), (1999): 395-413. https://doi.org/10.1080/10835547.1999.12091004.

Brasington, D. M., and Haurin, D. R. "Educational Outcome and House Value: A Test of the Value Added Approach." *Journal of Regional Science, 46*(2), (2006): 245-268. https://doi.org/10.1111/j.0022-4146.2006.00440.

Brasington, D. M., Hite, D., and Andres, J. "Housing Prices Impact of Racial, Income, Education, and Age Neighborhood Segregation." *Journal of Regional Science, 55*(3), (2015): 442-467. https://doi.org/10.1111/jors.12173.

Buck, S. *Acting White: The Ironic Legacy of Desegregation.* Yale University Press, 2010.

Bushrow-Cassidy, E. A., Sitarik, R. A., Havstad, S., Park, S., Bielak, F. L., Austin, C., Johnson, C., and Arora, M. "Burden of Higher Lead Exposure in African-Americans Starts in Utero and Persist into Childhood." *Environmental International,*

108, (2017): 221-227. https://dx.doi.org/10.1016%2Fj. envint.2017.08.021.

Carver-Thomas, D., and Hammond-Darling, L. *Teacher turnover: Why it matters and what we can do about it.* Learning Policy Institute, 2017. https://learningpolicyinstitute.org/sites/ default/files/product-files/Teacher_Turnover_REPORT. pdf.

Chua, A. *World on Fire: How Exporting Free Market Democracy Breeds Ethnic Hatred and Global Instability.* Anchor Books, 2004.

Cohen, S., Doyle, W. J., and Baum, A. "Socioeconomic Status is Associated With Stress Hormones." *Psychosomatic Medicine, 68*(3), (2006): 414-420. https://doi.org/10.1097/01. psy.0000221236.37158.b9.

Cooper, J. G., Kotval-K, Z., Kotval, Z., and Mullin, J. "University Community Partnerships." *Humanities, 3*, (2014): 88-101. https://doi.org/doi: 10.3390/h3010088.

Crouch, E. "East St. Louis School Board Cedes Control to State." *St. Louis Post Dispatch*, May 11, 2011. https://www. stltoday.com/news/local/education/east-st-louis-school- board-cedes-control-to-state/article_9402ecc5-e4a1-588d- bf17-05e31dc4b959.amp.html.

Cuddington, J. T. "Capital Flight: Estimates, Issues, and Explanations." *Princeton Studies in International Finance, 58*, (1986): 1-44. https://ies.princeton.edu/pdf/S58.pdf.

Davidson, A. "Is College Tuition Too High?" *New York Times*, September 8, 2015. https://www.nytimes.com/2015/09/13/ magazine/is-college-tuition-too-high.htm.

Day, J. K. *The Southern Manifesto: Massive Resistance and the Fight to Preserve Segregation.* University Press of Mississippi, 2015.

Eligon, J., and Gebeloff, R. "Affluent and Black, and Still Trapped by Segregation." *New York Times*, August 20, 2016. https://

www.nytimes.com/2016/08/21/us/milwaukee-segregation-wealthy-black-families.html.

Farah, M. J. "The Neuroscience of Socioeconomic Status: Correlates, Causes and Consequences." *Neuron, 96*(1), (2017): 56-71. https://doi.org/10.1016/j.neuron.2017.08.034.

Farah, M. J. "Socioeconomic Status and the Brain: Prospects for Neuroscience-informed Policy." *Neuroscience, 19*(7), (2018): 428-438. https://doi.org/10.1038/s41583-018-0023-2.

Fausto-Sterling, A. "Science Matters, Culture Matters." *Johns Hopkins University Press, 46*(1), (2003): 109-124. https://doi.org/10.1353/pbm.2003.0007.

Feng, H., and Lu, M. "School Quality and Housing Prices: Empirical Evidence From a Natural Experiment in Shanghai, China." *Journal of Housing Economics, 22*(4), (2013): 291-307. https://doi.org/10.1016/j.jhe.2013.10.003.

Fenwick, L. *Jim Crow's Pink Slip: The Untold Story of Black Principals and Teacher Leadership.* Harvard Education Press, 2022.

Firebaugh, G., and Acciai, F. "For Blacks in America, the Gap in Neighborhood Poverty has Declined Faster than Segregation." *Proceedings of the National Academy of Science of the United States of America,* 113(47), (2016):13372-13377. https://doi.org/10.1073/pnas.1607220113.

Fishback, P. V., Rose, J., and Snowden, K. *Well Worth Saving: How the New Deal Safeguarded Home Ownership.* University of Chicago Press, 2013.

Fordham, S., and Ogbu, J. U. "Black Students' School Success: Coping with the Burden of Acting White?" *The Urban Review, 18*(3), (1986): 176-296. https://psycnet.apa.org/doi/10.1007/BF01112192.

Frey, W. *Diversity Explosion: How New Racial Demographics are Remaking America.* Brookings Institution Press, 2014.

Grodzins, M. *The Metropolitan Area as a Racial Problem.* University of Pittsburgh Press, 1958.

Harris, D. R. "Property Values Drop When Blacks Move In, Because . . .: Racial and Socioeconomic Determinates of Neighborhood Desirability." *American Sociological Review,* *64*(3), (1999): 461-479. https://doi.org/10.2307/2657496.

Haushofer, J., de Laat, J. D., and Chemin, M. "Poverty Raises Levels of the Stress Hormone Cortisol: Evidence from Weather Shock in Kenya." Dartmouth University, 2012. https://www.dartmouth.edu/neudc2012/docs/paper_195. pdf.

Haushofer, J., and Fehr, E. "On the Psychology of Poverty." *American Association for the Advancement of Science, 344*(6186), (2014): 862-867. https://doi.org/ 10.1126/science.1232491.

Imberman, S. A., and Lovenheim, M. F. "Does the market value value-added? Evidence from housing prices after a public release of school and teacher value added." *Journal of Urban Economics, 91*(C), (2016): 104-121. https://doi.org/10.1016/j. jue.2015.06.001.

Isenberg, N. *White Trash: The 400-Year Untold History of Class in America.* Penguin Books, 2017.

Jackson, K. *Crabgrass Frontier: The Subordination of the United States.* Oxford University Press, 1985.

Jan, T. "The One Area Where Racial Disparities in Housing Have Disappeared." *Washington Post*, March 5, 2017. https:// www.washingtonpost.com/news/wonk/wp/2017/05/05/ the-one-area-where-racial-disparities-in-housing-has- disappeared/?utm_term=.be666eb947bd.

Jargowsky, P. A. "Concentration of poverty in the new millennium: Changes in prevalence, composition, and location of high poverty neighborhoods." The Century Foundation and Rutgers Center for Urban Research and Education, 2015. https://

production-tcf.imgix.net/app/uploads/2013/12/18013623/ Concentration_of_Poverty_in_the_New_Millennium-9.pdf.

Jenson, E. *Teaching With Poverty in Mind: What Being Poor Does to Kids' Brains and What Schools Can Do About It*. Association for Supervision & Curriculum Development, 2019.

Jenson, E. *Engaging Students with Poverty in Mind: Practical Strategies for Raising Achievement*. Association for Supervision & Curriculum Development, 2013.

Kamin, D. "Black Homeowners Face Discrimination in Appraisals." *New York Times*, August 25, 2020. https://www. nytimes.com/2020/08/25/realestate/blacks-minorities-appraisals-discrimination.html.

Kashian, R., and Rockwell, J. S. "Town and Gown: The Negative External of a University on Housing Prices." *Journal of Real Estate Practice and Education, 16*(1), (2013): 1-12. https://doi. org/10.1080/10835547.2013.12091716.

Katznelson, I. *When Affirmative Action was White: An Untold History of Racial Inequality in Twentieth-century America*. W. W. Norton, 2006.

Katznelson, I. *Fear Itself: The New Deal and the Origins of Our Time*. Liveright, 2014.

Kendi, I. X. *Stamped From the Beginning: The History of Racist Ideas in America*. Bold Type Books, 2017.

Kenner Commission. "National Advisory Commission on Civil Disorders, Report," 1967. https://www.ncjrs.gov/pdffiles1/ Digitization/8073NCJRS.pdf.

Kim, J. "Achieving Mixed Income Communities Through Infill? The Effect of Infill Housing on Neighborhood Income Diversity." *Journal of Urban Affairs, 38*(2), (2016): 280-297. https://doi.org/10.1111/juaf.12207.

King, M. L. *Where Do We Go From Here: Chaos or Community?* Beacon Press, 2010.

Kneebone, E. "Ferguson, Mo. Emblematic of Growing Suburban Poverty." Brookings Institute, 2014. https://www.brookings.edu/blog/the-avenue/2014/08/15/ferguson-mo-emblematic-of-growing-suburban-poverty/.

Kucheva, Y., and Sander, R. "The Misunderstood Consequence of *Shelley v. Kraemer*." *Social Science Research, 48,* (2014): 212-233. https://doi.org/10.1016/j.ssresearch.2014.06.007.

Kye, S. H. "The Persistence of White Flight in Middle Class Suburbia." *Social Science Research, 72*(1), (2018): 38-52. https://doi.org/10.1016/j.ssresearch.2018.02.005.

Lakoff, G., and Johnson, M. "The Metaphorical Structure of the Human Conceptual System." *Cognitive Science, 4*(2), (1980): 195-208. https://doi.org/10.1207/s15516709cog0402_4.

Landis, K. "Who Pays the Highest Property Taxes in the Metro-east? You Might Be Surprised." *Bellville News Democrat,* October 26, 2017. https://www.bnd.com/news/local/article181052031.html.

Leonce, N. "Causes and Effects of Capital Flight from Africa: Lessons From Case Studies." *African Development Review, 28*(1), (2016): 2-7. https://doi.org/10.1111/1467-8268.12177.

Levin, R., Brown, M. J., Kashtock, M. E., Jacobs, D. E., Whelan, E. A., Rodman, J., Schock, M. R., Padilla, A., and Sinks, T. "Lead Exposure in U.S. Children 2008: Implications for Prevention." *Environmental Health Perspective, 116*(10), (2008): 1285-1293. https://dx.doi.org/10.1289%2Fehp.11241.

Lipina, S. J. "Critical Consideration About the Use of Poverty Measures in the Study of Cognitive Development." *International Journal of Psychology, 52*(3), (2017): 241-250. https://doi.org/10.1002/ijop.12282.

Loewen, J. W. *Sundown Towns: A Hidden Dimension of American Racism.* The New Press, 2018.

Loving, C. A., Finke, S. M., and Salter, R. J. "Does Home Equality Explain the Black Wealth Gap?" *Journal of Housing and Built Environment, 27*(4), (2012): 427-451. https://doi.org/10.1007/s10901-011-9256-3.

Luhmann, N., and Gilgen, P. *Introduction to Systems Theory.* Polity, 2012.

Manis, M. A. *A Fire You Can't Put Out: The Civil Rights Life of Birmingham's Reverend Fred Shuttleworth.* University Alabama Press, 2001.

Massey, D. S., and Denton, N. A. *American Apartheid: Segregation and the Making of the Underclass.* Harvard University Press, 1993.

Massey, J., Field, S., and Chan, Y. "Partnering for economic development: How town-gown relations impact local economic development in small and medium cities." *Canadian Journal of Higher Education, 44*(2), (2014): 52-169. https://doi.org/10.47678/cjhe.v44i2.183813.

McKenna, P., and Lavelle, M. "This is an Emergency: 1 Million African Americans Live Near Oil, Gas Facilities." *Inside Climate News*, November 14, 2017. https://insideclimatenews.org/news/14112017/african-americans-exposed-oil-gas-wells-refineries-health-risks-naacp-study.

Mearman, A. "Critical Realism in Economic and Open-system Ontology: A Critique." *Review of Social Economy, 64*(1), (2006): 47-75. https://doi.org/10.1080/00346760500529955.

Mohai, P., and Saha, R. "Racial Inequality in the Distribution of Hazardous Waste: A National-Level Reassessment." *Social Problems, 54*(3), (2007): 343-370. https://doi.org/10.1525/sp.2007.54.3.343.

Mohai, P., and Saha, R. "Which came first, people or pollution? Assessing the disparate siting and post-siting demographic change hypotheses of environmental injustice." *Environmental*

Research Letters, 10(11), 2015. https://iopscience.iop.org/article/10.1088/1748-9326/10/11/115008/pdf.

Moody, H., Darden, J. T., and Pigozzi, B. W. "The Racial Gap in Childhood Blood Lead Levels Related to Socioeconomic Positions of Residence in Metropolitan Detroit." *Sociology of Race and Ethnicity, 2*(2), (2016): 200-218. https://doi.org/10.1177%2F23326492215608873.

Myrdal, G. *An American Dilemma: The Negro Problem and Modern Democracy*, Vol. I. Routledge, 1944.

National Center for Education Statistics. "The Illinois Data for Fiscal and Instructional Results, Study, and Transparency (Illinois Data FIRST) Project," 2015. https://nces.ed.gov/programs/slds/state.asp?stateabbr=IL.

National Center for Education Statistics, 2015. https://nces.ed.gov/programs/slds/state.asp?stateabbr=IL.

National Center for Education Statistics, 2020. https://nces.ed.gov/pubs2020/2020303.pdf.

National Commission on Excellence in Education, 1983. "A Nation at Risk: The Imperative for Educational Reform." https://www.edreform.com/wp-content/uploads/2013/02/A_Nation_At_Risk_1983.pdf.

National Fair Housing Alliance. "The Case for Fair Housing: 2017 Fair Housing Trends Report." https://nationalfairhousing.org/wp-content/uploads/2017/07/TRENDS-REPORT-2017-FINAL.pdf.

National Student Clearinghouse Research Center, 2016. "National College Progression Rates for High Schools Participating in the National Student Clearinghouse StudentTracker Service." https://nscresearchcenter.org/hsbenchmarks2016/.

National Student Clearinghouse Research Center. "Completing College—National by Race and Ethnicity—2017." https://nscresearchcenter.org/signaturereport12-supplement-2/.

Paige, R., and Witty, E. *The Black-White Achievement Gap: Why Closing it is the Greatest Civil Rights Issue of Our Time.* AMACOM, 2010.

Parker, M. "After 32 years of HUD oversight, problems persist in East St. Louis public housing residents say." *Southern Illinoisan,* 2017. https://thesouthern.com/news/local/acha/after-years-of-hud-oversight-problems-persist-in-east-st/article_ac048f32-3234-570c-aa93-bb1bc4bdbdcd.html.

Pell Institute. "Indicators for Higher Education Equity in the United States," 2016. http://www.pellinstitute.org/downloads/publications-Indicators_of_Higher_Education_Equity_in_the_US_2016_Historical_Trend_Report.pdf.

Perkins, K. L., and Sampson, R. J. "Compounded Deprivation in the Transition to Adulthood: The Intersection of Racial and Economic Inequality Among Chicagoans, 1995-2013." *The Russell Sage Foundation Journal of the Social Sciences, 1*(1), (2015): 35-54. https://doi.org/10.7758/RSF.2015.1.1.03.

Rothstein, R. "The Making of Ferguson: Public Policies at the Root of its Troubles," Economic Policy Institute, 2014. https://www.epi.org/files/2014/making-of-ferguson-final.pdf.

Rothstein, R. *The Color of Law: The Forgotten History of How our Government Segregated America.* Liveright, 2017.

Sampson, R. J., and Winter, A. "The Racial Ecology of Lead Poisoning: Toxic Inequality in Chicago Neighborhoods, 1995-2013." *Du Bois Review, Social Science Research, 13*(2), (2016): 261-283. https://doi.org/10.1017/S1742058X16000151.

Shapoval, I. A. "Subjective Quality of Life in the Psychology of Poverty." *Moscow State University of Psychology and Education, 6*(4), (2015): 207-218. https://doi.org/10.17759/psyedu.2014060418.

Sowell, T. *Basic Economics: A Common Sense Guide to the Economy.* Basic Books, 2014.

Sowell, T. *Discrimination and Disparities.* Basic Books, 2018.

Spady, W. "Dropouts From Higher Education: Toward an Empirical Model." *Interchange, 2*(3), (1971): 38-62. https://doi.org/10.1007/BF02282469.

Spellings, M. "A Test of Leadership: Charting the Future of U.S. Higher Education." U.S. Department of Education, 2006. https://www2.ed.gov/about/bdscomm/list/hiedfuture/reports/pre-pub-report.pdf.

St. John, E. P., Duan-Barnett, N., and Moronski-Chapman, K. M. *Public Policy and Higher Education: Reframing Strategies for Preparation, Access, and College Success.* Routledge, 2013.

Sugrue, T. *The Origins of the Urban Crisis: Race and Inequality in Post-war Detroit.* Princeton University, 1996.

Tinto, V. "Dropout From Higher Education: A Theoretical Synthesis of Recent Research." *Review of Educational Research, 45*(1), (1975): 89-125. https://doi.org/10.3102%2F003465543045001089.

Townsend, L. "How Universities Successfully Retain and Graduate Black Students." *Journal of Black Higher Education, 4,* (1994): 85-89. https://doi.org/10.2307/2963380.

Vanegrift, D., Lockshiss, A., and Lahr, M. "Town versus Gown: The Effect of a College on Housing Prices and the Tax Base." *Growth and Change, 43*(2), (2012): 304-344. https://doi.org/10.1111/j.1468-2257.2012.00587.x.

von Bertalanffy, L. "The History and Status of General Systems Theory." *The Academy of Management Journal, 15*(4), (1972): 407-426. https://doi.org/10.2307/255139.

von Stumm, S., and Plomin, R. "Socioeconomic Status and the Growth of Intelligence from Infancy Through Adolescence."

Intelligence, 48, (2015): 30-36. https://doi.org/10.1016/j.intell.2014.10.002.

Wallis, E. S., and Valentinov, V. "The imperviance of conceptual systems: Cognitive and moral aspects." *Kybernetes, 45*(9), (2016): 1437-1451. https://doi.org/10.1108/K-04-2016-0072.

Wen, H., Xiao, Y., Hui, E., and Zhang, L. "Education quality, accessibility, and housing price: Does spatial heterogeneity exist in education capitalization?" *Habitat International, 78*, (2018): 68-82. https://doi.org/10.1016/j.habitatint.2018.05.012.

Wilson, W. J. *The Declining Significance of Race: Blacks and Changing American Institutions*. University of Chicago Press, 1978.

Wilson, W. J. *The Truly Disadvantaged: The Inner City, the Underclass, and Public Policy*. University of Chicago Press, 1987.

Wisely, J. "Flint Residents Paid America's Highest Water Rates." *Detroit Free Press*, February 16, 2016. https://www.freep.com/story/news/local/michigan/flint-water-crisis/2016/02/16/study-flint-paid-highest-rate-us-water/80461288/.

Zeitz, J. *Building the Great Society: Inside Lyndon Johnson's White House*. Viking, 2018.

About the Author

Dr. Monica Shepherd is an Illinois native. She is a history professor and research methodologist. Dr. Shepherd's interests cover economic methodology, public policy, and academic theory. In part, her research focuses on social pathologies in disadvantaged communities and education policy. She can be reached at MonicaShephard.com

Review Requested:

We'd like to know if you enjoyed the book.
Please consider leaving a review on the platform
from which you purchased the book.

www.ingramcontent.com/pod-product-compliance
Lightning Source LLC
Chambersburg PA
CBHW051214250726
48655CB00006B/2410